History of the Tennessee Society of Certified Public Accountants

Volume II, 1978-2014

Enhancing the success of our members through service, support and advocacy

History of the Tennessee Society of Certified Public Accountants
Volume II, 1978-2014.

ISBN 9780692416655.

©2015. All Rights Reserved.

Tennessee Society of Certified Public Accountants
201 Powell Place
Brentwood, TN 37027

In appreciation of the leadership provided by all of the TSCPA officers, directors and staff who have served the Society with distinction.

Contents

Author's Note	4
Introduction	5
1. Laying the Foundations of a Profession: 1978-1986	7
2. The Profession Polices Itself: 1987-1992	31
3. Building For the Future: 1993-1996	53
4. Vision and Growth: 1997-2001	71
5. Wreck and Recovery: 2001-2004	95
6. Expanding Possibilities: 2005-2009	111
7. Developing the Next Generation: 2009-2014	129
Summary, Conclusions and Observations	149
Appendices	152

Author's Note

Regarding my role in this book, the adage "never ask for something you want, you might get it" applies. While I was researching for a presentation to celebrate the 75th anniversary of the Appalachian Chapter, TSCPA President and CEO Brad Floyd asked if I was willing to compile a second volume of the TSCPA history, from 1978 to 2014. I agreed. The main problem I have faced in penning this book was exactly the opposite of the problem facing Harold O. Wilson and Hilary H. Osborn, the authors of Volume 1 of this history. While their problem was having too little (or missing) information, my problem has been having too much information. This information overload has primarily occurred since the early 1980s, with the increased use of computers and the ease in which information is prepared, saved and shared. I have attempted to capture the world in which Tennessee CPAs have operated over the last 36 years, a world driven by technology and change.

I would like to thank the TSCPA communications team, for serving as editors extraordinaire. They added greatly to the content, format and readability of the book. The entire Society staff also deserves thanks for their assistance in gathering the voluminous information that provided the content for this book. They located, scanned and copied pages upon pages of documents and never complained about my intrusion into their daily work.

I would like to thank Brad Floyd for his tremendous guidance in writing this book and his outstanding leadership of the Society. Brad has been and continues to be the guiding force of the Society and, along with the other staff members, is the primary reason TSCPA is one of the leading CPA societies in the country.

Thanks to my children, John and Samantha, for understanding all the times I was gone to attend meetings, workshops, conventions and other Society activities, and also to Jacqui for holding down the fort in my absence.

The Society has been a big part of mine and many others' lives, and lifelong friendships have been formed from my participation over the last 30 or so years. I hope I have captured the times and brought back some fond memories for the readers.

—Mark E. Steadman, Ph.D., CPA, CGMA
Johnson City

Dr. Steadman is professor of accountancy at East Tennessee State University. He is past president of TSCPA's Appalachian Chapter and has served as a member of the TSCPA Council and Board of Directors. He is also a past recipient of TSCPA's Educator of the Year Award and Committee Chair of the Year Award.

Introduction

This book is a continuation of *History of the Tennessee Society of Certified Public Accountants 1904-1977*, authored by Dr. Harold O. Wilson and Hilary H. Osborn. Their book, published by TSCPA in 1977, details the early formation of the profession and its development in Tennessee. A brief summary of their work follows:

The public accounting profession in the United States was first organized in New York. Early leaders of the profession lobbied the New York State Legislature, and the original CPA bill was passed in April 1896. In Tennessee, the early efforts to form a professional organization were located in Memphis. An application for a Charter of Incorporation was filed on Jan. 29, 1904, with the County Court Clerk of Shelby County. The incorporators of the Society (then known as the Tennessee Society of Public Accountants) were Edward S. Elliott, Andrew Sam Hull, Charles Flisher, W.L. McFarland and Frank Goodman.

Following the model in New York, legislation was filed to recognize certified public accountants in 1905, 1907 and 1910. This legislation failed to get out of committee each time. Finally, a bill to create the state-recognized certification was passed in 1913. Challenges to the bill continued until 1935, when a newer version of the bill was passed that in effect ended all opposition to the issue. In 1928, a name change charter was filed, and the Tennessee Society of Certified Public Accountants became the official name of the group. Chapters were formed, state governance bylaws and policies were passed, officers were elected, and the organization began to operate on a permanent basis.

The first Board of Directors meeting was held on Aug. 8, 1931, at the Andrew Jackson Hotel in Nashville. This meeting has evolved into the annual meeting of the Society, held at the state convention.

In October 1966, TSCPA moved into a new office space in the Frost Building, at 161 8th Ave. N. in Nashville. This was the first permanent office location to be used exclusively for Society functions. Dr. Axel Swang served as Executive Secretary from 1957 to 1968. Nels T. "Ted"

Moody was hired on Aug. 21, 1967, and served as the first full-time Executive Director until his retirement in August 1987.

The first annual committee day was held on Aug. 17, 1969, and was deemed to be a huge success. All 24 of the Society's committees met to review past accomplishments and plans for the future. For many years, the committee day was organized into an annual Leadership Conference.

In June 1974, the Tennessee State Board of Accountancy announced that beginning immediately, applicants for the CPA exam would be required to have obtained a college degree prior to sitting for the exam.

One additional item that occurred in the 1970s greatly influenced the accountancy profession in Tennessee and must be addressed. Through the first 50 years of professional recognition, continuing professional education (CPE) for CPAs was not required by either the state board of accountancy or TSCPA. In 1975, TSCPA began a voluntary CPE program. The program called for 56 hours to be earned in a 2-year period, with 24 hours required in 1975 as a phase-in of the program. Even though it was not required by law or policy, 34 percent of TSCPA members completed this requirement. This program would be expanded and mandated by the state board in the future.

According to a 1976 research monograph by Robert E. Guinn published by Middle Tennessee State University's Business and Economic Research Center, the service mix for CPA firms in Tennessee at that time was: bookkeeping, 17.7 percent; auditing opinion, 25.9 percent; auditing (unaudited), 21.1 percent; tax, 27.4 percent; management services, 6.4 percent; and other, 1.6 percent.

In October 1977, B. Bradford Floyd was hired by the Society as the Administrative Service Manager. A graduate of the University of Florida, Floyd joined the TSCPA staff after serving on the staff of the Florida Institute of CPAs. He was appointed TSCPA Executive Director in August 1987, and he continues to serve today as TSCPA President and CEO.

CHAPTER ONE
1978-1986

Laying the Foundations of a Profession

In 1978, Jimmy Carter was president and the nation was still reeling from Watergate and the resignation of President Nixon. Top news stories included Love Canal, Jonestown and Son of Sam. Gas was 79 cents per gallon, a pound of bacon cost $1.20 and New York strip steak was $2.39 per pound. The Dow Jones Industrial Average closed the year at 805. Popular TV shows included *Dallas*, *M*A*S*H*, *Happy Days* and *The Waltons*. The disco era was in full swing, with the Bee Gees leading the charts ("Night Fever," "Stayin' Alive"), while Debby Boone ("You Light Up My Life") and Barry Manilow ("Can't Smile Without You") provided the softer sound for the year. The most popular movies were *Animal House*, *Grease* and *Halloween*. The Dallas Cowboys beat the Denver Broncos 27-10 in Super Bowl XII.

John R. McCabe Jr. of Memphis served as TSCPA president for the 1977-78 year. According to a Missouri Management of Accounting Conference, partners in CPA firms were billing an average of $33-44 per hour, while staff were billed out at $21 per hour. As the

TSCPA President 1978-79
John R. McCabe Jr.

profession entered the late 1970s, CPAs were primarily performing audit and tax services, and in early 1978, the American Institute of Certified Public Accountants (AICPA) introduced standards for unaudited financial statements. The Institute proposed services that would benefit the needs of private companies for different levels of accounting services. Compilation and review services were proposed by the AICPA Accounting and Review Services Committee. Once implemented, these standards provided CPA firms with expanded service opportunities.

Another issue undertaken by the AICPA was the elimination of the 50-year-old ban on advertising and client solicitation. For the first time, CPAs were allowed to advertise, as long as the message was not "false, misleading or deceptive." The new rule did not prohibit the direct, uninvited solicitation of a specific potential client.

In a survey discussed in the June 1978 *Tennessee CPA*, the major problems facing the CPA profession, many of which still affect CPAs today, were listed as:
- Government pressure (68 percent).
- Increased litigation involving CPA firms (41 percent).
- A declining level of public confidence in the profession (36 percent).
- Concerns about the effectiveness of self-regulation (28 percent).
- Potential conflicts of interest arising from CPA firms offering management advisory services (24 percent).
- Lack of unanimity within the profession (18 percent).
- Maintaining a commitment to independence (15 percent).
- An inability to recruit topflight talent (11 percent).

In March 1978, the TSCPA Educational and Memorial Foundation (EMF) started the Life Associate Program. This program recognized CPAs who contributed $500 over a five-year period in order to fund scholarships for accounting students in Tennessee. The foundation offered 42 CPE programs in 1978, for total revenue of $94,274. As of

February 1978, TSCPA had 2,048 dues-paying members and 39 Life Members. The financial statements that year showed total Society revenue of $269,751, total expenses of $238,259 and a total fund balance of $120,406.

Nationally, the accounting profession was under increased scrutiny from the federal government. Financial scandals in the mid-1970s had led to several Congressional investigations. Perhaps the most scathing result was the publication from the Senate Committee on Government Operations, *The Accounting Establishment*, in December 1976 (also known as the Metcalf Report). This study examined the structure of the entire profession (including the AICPA, FASB, the SEC and other groups) and the influence the Big Eight accounting firms had in controlling this structure. The study contained the infamous quote "The 'Big Eight' are often called 'public accounting firms' or 'independent public accounting firms.' This study finds little evidence that they either serve the public or that they are independent in fact from the interests of their corporate clients." The study concluded with recommendations that would have amounted to a complete federal government takeover of the profession, including establishing both accounting and auditing standards. The AICPA's and state societies' reaction to the study was to focus on self-regulatory actions that would ease the threat of this takeover.

> The Life Associate Program recognized CPAs who contributed $500 over a five-year period in order to fund scholarships for accounting students in Tennessee.

In Tennessee, TSCPA took the lead in this renewed emphasis on self-regulation. The first point of concern was the Tennessee State Board of Accountancy. The Board of Accountancy was due to sunset on June 30, 1980, and the 1978 state legislature had not passed an acceptable accountancy law. The 1978 version of the Tennessee

Accountancy Act would have granted public accountants (PAs) a CPA certificate without further demonstrating their competence, and TSCPA was strongly opposed to that proposal.

In order to strengthen the TSCPA government relations program, a group of CPAs met at the Hilton Airport Inn in Nashville to form the Tennessee CPA Political Action Committee (PAC) on March 28, 1978. Members present were Joe Kraft, Darrel Tongate, Herman Bradley, Charles Breeding, Paul Gurley and Dan Johnson. The group passed a resolution that those present constituted the initial trustees of the Tennessee CPA Political Action Committee, Inc. Bylaws had been prepared by legal counsel and were adopted unanimously. Initial officers, elected by acclamation, were Joe Kraft (chairman), Herman Bradley (vice chairman) and Darrel Tongate (secretary-treasurer). A letter of fund solicitation was mailed to all CPAs in April 1978 stressing the importance of CPA involvement in the Tennessee legislative process. In order to support good government by making campaign contributions to qualified candidates for the state legislature, the PAC asked for a $50 donation from each TSCPA member. The trustees asked all CPAs to be involved in this process in order to support candidates that understood this important public interest issue. The letter asked, "Only you realize the investment of time, money and just plain hard work expended in order to receive your certificate. Do you feel a $50 contribution is too high a price to protect your profession?"

On Jan. 8, 1979, the TSCPA bylaws were amended to establish a provisional member category for those individuals who had passed the CPA exam but not yet earned their license.

The 48th Annual Convention was held Aug. 6-8, 1978, at the Chattanooga Choo-Choo and Hilton Inn. Committee day was held Sept. 9, 1978, in Nashville. A total of 24 committees met that day, and issues discussed included an evaluation of TSCPA bylaws, career counseling for high school students, improvements to the *Tennessee CPA* newsletter and proposed mandatory CPE.

On June 18, 1979, the Upper Cumberland Chapter was formed, with Ed Lansford elected as the chapter's first president. The chapter consisted of CPAs located in Clay, Cumberland, DeKalb, Fentress, Jackson, Macon, Overton, Pickett, Putnam, Smith, Trousdale, Van Buren and White counties.

In 1979, James T. Thompson, a professor at Memphis State University, became the first CPA not employed in public accounting to be appointed to the Tennessee State Board of Accountancy.

During this period, public accountants were licensed in Tennessee to provide substantially the same services as CPAs; however, the educational and examination requirements were lower for PAs. Sen. John Hicks was a public accountant in Tennessee who also happened to be an influential senior senator. There were no CPAs serving in the state legislature at the time, which provided the Tennessee Association of Public Accountants with substantially more influence than TSCPA, even though there were many more CPAs licensed in Tennessee than PAs.

TSCPA President 1979-80
Maxie O. Patton

The TSCPA Executive Committee met at the Hilton Airport Inn in Nashville on Aug. 17, 1979. President Maxie Patton, of Nashville, presided over the meeting. The chairman of the Government Relations Committee, Douglas T. Smith, presented a report on the committee's activity with regard to the new accountancy law. Two meetings had been held with PAs by the TSCPA "Negotiating Committee," comprised of Douglas Smith, Joe Kraft, Herman Bradley and William Puryear. The sessions were held on July 23 and Aug. 13. Smith stated that he was seeking Executive Committee approval of the following plan of action:

1. Further refine the draft of the bill and meet with the PAs again.

2. Get assurances from the PAs, Sen. John Hicks, Speaker Ned McWherter and Lt. Gov. John Wilder that they would support the bill.
3. Call a special meeting of Council.

John McCabe moved that the plan be approved, and the motion was seconded. A 90-minute discussion then ensued about the plan. The general consensus was that the bill, if passed as drafted, would further denigrate the public interest, but a greater damage would be done if the State Board of Accountancy was allowed to expire. The motion passed with the required two-thirds majority.

Additional items were discussed at the meeting. James E. Totherow was recognized as the Upper Cumberland representative on the Executive Committee. Nels T. "Ted" Moody, Executive Director, also discussed office space and computer services. Moody stated that the lease on the present headquarters would expire on Sept. 30, 1981, and that more space was needed. Additional office space was also a major concern of Moody's. He concluded that it may be wise to consider moving before the present lease expired. Computer service was noted as being marginally acceptable and becoming more expensive.

On Aug. 18, 1979, the Long-Range Planning Committee met to discuss future operational issues confronting the Society. The committee voted to recommend that a Peer Review Committee be added to the current committee structure. The committee voted to recommend that the present Executive Committee be replaced by a nine-person Board of Directors that would be elected by Council for three-year terms, with three members representing each grand division of the state. The committee concluded that additional study was needed in order to determine the need for a chief operating officer who was a member of the accounting profession. Finally, the unanimous consent of the committee was that the Society should be prepared to move to larger headquarters in the very near future, and consideration should be given to owning rather than leasing the space. It also recommended that a Standing Committee be formed to consider personnel and office facility matters on a routine basis.

The Scholarship Committee had surveyed accounting professors across the state during 1979 in order to reorganize their process of awarding scholarships. New guidelines were established for the 1979-80 academic year to be used to award the grants. The guidelines were academic achievement (50 percent), essay and recommendations (20 percent), financial need (20 percent) and leadership (10 percent). The committee awarded 12 scholarships totaling $6,000. In a memo to the Executive Committee dated Nov. 9, 1979, Government Relations Committee Chair Douglas Smith stated that the new accountancy act had been approved by the Tennessee Association of Public Accountants (TAPA) and by the TSCPA Government Relations Committee. Smith indicated that he was going to present the issue at the Council meeting on Dec. 1. The proposed bill was a compromise with the PAs, but Smith believed that it was an improvement in the accounting law.

The Dec. 1, 1979, interim Council meeting was held at the Nashville Hilton Airport Inn, with President Maxie Patton presiding. At the time, the Society had a total membership of 2,457. Council approved a resolution that the Society would make a $100 contribution in the name of each deceased member to the Educational and Memorial Foundation and advise the next of kin that a contribution had been made. Douglas Smith presented the draft of the proposed new accountancy law, which was approved unanimously. Bill Puryear moved that a resolution of appreciation be adopted to recognize Smith for his leadership as chair of the Government Relations Committee. The motion passed unanimously. With a standing ovation, the Council also expressed their appreciation of the efforts of Bill Puryear, Joe Kraft, Herman Bradley and Maxie Patton for their work in the development of the new bill.

Additionally, James Thompson, Chair of the Educational Standards Committee, suggested that the formal acceptance of standards for formal group study and self-study CPE be deferred until further consideration could be made by the Continuing Professional Education Committee. J.P. Foster, Chair of the Professional Ethics Committee, spoke to Council and emphasized the need to restructure the committee. Administrative procedures to preserve records of actions taken by the committee were needed. The president commented that the Bylaws Committee would consider these suggestions.

> On Dec. 1, 1979, the Society had a total membership of 2,457.

Joe Kraft reported that the Educational and Memorial Foundation was alive, but not very well, and that it needed more money. There were 46 Life Associates of the foundation at the time.

As the 1980 legislative session opened, the new accountancy act was at the forefront of the leadership's radar. The act contained provisions that mandated continuing education, rules of professional conduct and revisions to licensing and registration requirements for CPAs. The proposed act had been agreed upon by both TSCPA and the TAPA, yet, as it moved through the legislative process, amendments were being proposed in the Senate. The Executive Committee held a conference call on Jan. 18, 1980, to discuss these amendments. Douglas Smith reported to the committee that Sen. John Hicks planned to amend the agreed-to bill to exclude from CPE requirements all persons over age 55. Also, an amendment requiring a state-chartered organization to obtain an accountant's report prepared by a CPA would allow a PA's report to meet this requirement. The Executive Committee unanimously opposed these amendments as violations of the public interest that were unconstitutional as a violation of the right of private contract.

On Feb. 6, a second conference call of the Executive Committee was held. Douglas Smith advised the committee that the proposed bill was being considered in the Senate Government Operations Committee the next day, but he did not know the number of amendments or the specific wording of any amendments until they were presented for consideration. The bill's sponsor, Sen. Ben Atchley, of Knoxville, had asked TSCPA for their position on any amendments to the bill. The Executive Committee re-affirmed their position to support the agreed-upon bill. However, if an amendment was made that would interfere with any organization's right to choose an accountant, it would be vigorously opposed by TSCPA. To a lesser extent, if the amendment to weaken the CPE system was introduced, the Society would be willing to consider additional options. The legislation was passed without amendment in April 1980 and would provide the basic foundation for state regulation of CPAs that still stands today.

The act required 120 hours of CPE every three years for CPAs. The experience requirement was established as two years if serving under a CPA or three years' experience satisfactory to the Board if working under a non-CPA. A master's degree would count as one year experience in either circumstance. Senator Atchley was the primary sponsor of accountancy-related legislation in the Tennessee General Assembly in the 1980s and 1990s. He served as the Senate's Republican leader for over 20 years, and was a great friend to the CPA profession during that time.

Now that the Society leadership had successfully passed the new Accountancy Act, their actions turned toward revising the internal operations of the organization. Council met on June 9, 1980, at the Hyatt Regency in Memphis and considered many action items. Officers were elected, auditors were selected and committee updates were given. James Thompson reported on behalf of the Educational Standards Committee. After his presentation, Council passed a resolution to adopt the AICPA Statement on Standards for Formal Group and Formal Self-Study Programs as the standards for Society-sponsored CPE, and to recommend that the State Board of Accountancy adopt the same standards. The Long-Range Planning Committee reported that they were studying a proposed restructuring of the Society. The Office Personnel & Management Advisory Committee stated they were still in the process of evaluating office space, computer needs and staff compensation plans. Finally, President Patton commented that the Bylaws Committee had submitted a draft of completely revised bylaws that would be reviewed by the Executive Committee and several other committees for consideration.

President Truman Brooks, of Chattanooga, presided over the Aug. 4, 1980, Executive Committee meeting at the Airport Hilton Inn in Nashville. Although all members of the State Board of Accountancy had not yet been named, the committee approved forwarding the AICPA Statement on Standards for Formal Group and Formal Self-Study Programs, along with suggestions on how to implement the new CPE requirements, to the Board. The committee discussed the bylaws draft, and several suggestions were made to improve it. Office space was addressed again, with a motion being passed to approve $2,500 for professional services related to the acquisition of a permanent headquarters. The current office lease was set to expire in September, so the committee voted to expand to include the second floor at the current location. The position of receptionist-typist was approved, and the budget was amended to reflect the addition.

TSCPA President 1980-81
Truman W. Brooks

The Executive Committee met on Dec. 12, 1980, at the Hilton Airport Inn in Nashville. The committee voted to enter into a new employment agreement with Executive Director Ted Moody.

The interim Council meeting was held the next day at the Hilton Airport Inn in Nashville. A motion was approved to submit the bylaws amendments to the membership for approval, but only after the president appointed a new Bylaws Committee. This committee was to be composed of Society past presidents who were willing to serve. They would report to the Council at the December 1981 interim meeting. James Thompson, Chair of the Educational Standards

Committee, reported that they had completed the reporting of the Society voluntary program. The committee was also working closely with the State Board of Accountancy in implementing the new, required CPE program.

The early days of the newly organized State Board of Accountancy were not going smoothly. The position of executive director of the TSBA, created by the 1980 Accountancy Act, had not yet been filled by the Commissioner of Insurance. In April 1981, Grady Williams, state board chair, solicited the assistance of TSCPA in evaluating CPE courses, preparing forms for CPE, and developing forms to register firms, including the designation of a resident manager. Williams also asked Gov. Lamar Alexander to fill the executive director position immediately or a "chaotic situation may develop which would cause considerable harm to our profession."

The Executive Committee met on May 15, 1981, at the Hilton Airport Inn in Nashville. Douglas Smith, Chair of the Government Relations Committee, updated the group on the status of legislation and the results of a member survey on continuing professional education. The Executive Committee noted that the mandatory state board rules requiring CPE were in the rule-making process, and such rules would automatically override those of TSCPA.

Council met at the Hyatt in Hilton Head, S.C., on June 8, 1981. President Truman Brooks called the meeting to order. President-elect Tom Burgess noted that two ad hoc committees had been formed: one to study the Society's membership in the Southern States Conference of CPAs, an organization of southeastern states established to help promote cooperation and collaboration among its members at a time when state society resources were very sparse, and the other to study TSCPA committee functions and structure.

The Dec. 2, 1981, Executive Committee meeting focused on the proposed change in the bylaws. The group discussed the revised bylaws and passed a motion that they should be brought before Council for approval. Minutes of the meeting also reveal the "micromanaging" style of the committee during this time period.

Several small amendments to the budget were made that today would be considered immaterial and the responsibility of staff. On Dec. 5, the Council met and approved the bylaws change. They called for a ballot to be mailed to every member to approve or reject the proposal. If adopted by the membership, the new bylaws would become effective Feb. 1, 1982. The new bylaws were passed by membership, and they would be used by TSCPA in most major areas for the next 30 years. In May 1982, the Executive Committee requested the Finance Committee assess the needs of the Society with regard to a data processor (and programs) and the acquisition of a Society headquarters. The last meeting of the Executive Committee (the new bylaws called for the group to become the Board of Directors) was held on June 27, 1982. The group voted to recommend to Council that the Society use $52,000 of reserve funds to purchase a Wang data processor with the necessary programs. They also approved signing a five-year lease at the present office location and $16,000 for remodeling and furniture.

TSCPA President 1981-82
Thomas L. Burgess

On June 28, 1982, TSCPA Council met in Nashville, with President Thomas Burgess, of Nashville, presiding. Council approved the purchase of the data processor and remodeling proposals. The group also reviewed the revised policies of Council mandated by the new bylaws. William Sharp, Educational and Memorial Foundation President, urged all Council members to become Life Associates of the foundation.

On June 30, 1982, the Board of Directors held an organizational meeting, with the new president, Imogene Posey, of Knoxville, presiding. Posey became the first woman, as well as the first person from academia, to serve as president. At the Dec. 11 interim Council meeting, James Thompson, Chair of the TSBA, reiterated the state board's slow-moving nature and emphasized the need for cooperation between the state board and the Society. Also, Council voted unanimously to withdraw from the Southern States Conference of CPAs.

The May 5, 1983, Board of Directors meeting featured approval of several amendments to Council policies. Chapters were encouraged to offer CPE at their monthly meetings. The rules for the annual meeting and convention were updated to state that CPE would be developed by a technical program committee appointed by the president, but chapters were responsible for the social program, schedule, promotion and all other arrangements. Chapters were responsible for any excess expenses associated with the convention. The Board also clarified who had the authority to speak for the Society (members of Council, the Board of Directors and the president). Council approved these changes in June.

TSCPA President 1982-83
Imogene A. Posey

> Posey became the first woman, as well as the first person from academia, to serve as president.

Calvin A. King, of Memphis, served as president during 1983-84. Minutes of the Board of Directors and Council meetings during this time show that no pressing issues were facing the Society. In September 1983, the Board did authorize the Public Relations Committee to proceed with the Public Service Award program. The Board also authorized a $10,000 expenditure to upgrade the fixed

TSCPA President 1983-84
Calvin A. King

Imogene Posey presides at a meeting in Washington, D.C., between members of the Tennessee Congressional delegation, the TSCPA Board of Directors and key legislative contacts to discuss issues of importance to the CPA profession.

disc computer storage capacity from 16 MB to 32 MB, as well as other office improvements. The first Annual Accounting and Auditing Conference was held on Nov. 7-8 at the Opryland Hotel and was deemed a success. At the Dec. 3, 1983, Council meeting, William R. Carrigan and Marie E. Dubke commented in support of the AICPA proposal requiring a five-year degree to enter the profession.

TSCPA President 1984-85
C. Mack Browder

In May 1984, the society's publication, the *Tennessee CPA*, unveiled a new and much improved format. Since its inception, the monthly newsletter mailed to all members was fairly basic, black and white, and contained more technical information than Society news. The new publication featured color photos and a contemporary look.

The Board of Directors, led by President C. Mack Browder, of Memphis, met on May 2, 1984, at the Society office. The first order of business was to a budget amendment of $3,000 to pay the current year's auditor. Various CPA firms in Nashville had been doing the audit pro bono for years, but the growth of the Society, the EMF and the chapters had made the job too big for charity anymore.

Council met in the Civic Center in Jackson in June 1984. Very little business was conducted, but the minutes reflected that a notable individual had passed away earlier that month, Hilary H. Osborn, the co-author of Volume 1 of *The History of the Tennessee Society of Certified Public Accountants*. As in the previous year, the Society was operating in a fairly smooth manner with little controversy.

In July 1984, Anne Darnall, administrator of the TSBA, received a letter from the Bureau of Competition of the Federal Trade Commission (FTC) informing the TSBA that the agency was opening an investigation of the board's restrictions on advertising

President Mack Browder (far right) meets with members of the TSCPA Council (from left) Joe Decosimo, Lawson Crain and Henry Hoss.

and solicitation. A second letter was sent to the attorney general of Tennessee. The FTC was concerned that restrictions on competitive activity by state-licensed professionals might unreasonably restrain competition and injure consumers. At the September TSCPA Board of Directors meeting, Robert Brannon (a member of the TSBA) reported this investigation. The TSBA would eventually change their rules to allow CPAs to advertise and solicit clients in line with the AICPA language. At the same meeting, Douglas Smith reported that the Government Relations Committee was monitoring other states and was weighing the pros and cons of a "two tier" licensing system and the post-baccalaureate degree requirement. He emphasized that a position paper should be developed for key persons as soon as TSCPA policy was determined.

> In a memo to the Board of Directors dated Feb. 2, 1985, Moody requested the Board approve moving the Society office to 2000 Richard Jones Road in Green Hills.

On Dec. 5, 1984, Union Planters Bank officials advised the Society that they would like to occupy all the office space at 3904 Hillsboro Road, the location of the Society's office, by May 1, 1985. The Board of Directors met on Dec. 7 at the Hilton Airport Inn and discussed the office situation. President Browder indicated he would contact the chair of the ad hoc committee considering office facilities and ask if a report could be received from the committee by Jan. 15, 1985. In a memo to the Board of Directors dated Feb. 2, 1985, Moody requested the Board approve moving the Society office to 2000 Richard Jones Road in Green Hills. The Office Facilities Subcommittee of the Long-Range Planning Committee had concluded that it was not the time to consider a permanent location. The Green Hills location was available on a short-term lease and would be suitable until a permanent location could be identified. The Board approved the move in a conference call held Feb. 8, 1985.

On April 4, 1985, J. George Griesbeck, of Memphis, passed away at the age of 91. Mr. Griesbeck was a leading CPA in Memphis whose son and five grandsons were all certified public accountants. Two of his grandsons, Billy and John, would later serve as TSCPA presidents.

The first Board of Directors meeting held in the new office space took place on May 10, 1985. Once again, the accountancy law was the main topic of discussion. The TSBA was scheduled to be reviewed in the fall as part of the sunset law, and legislation would be introduced in 1986 to continue the Board. Douglas Smith suggested that TSCPA form a committee to provide a liaison with the TSBA during this process. President Browder agreed to form an ad hoc committee, and President-elect Lawson Crain agreed to continue the committee during his tenure.

Bob Brannon, Chair of the TSBA, reported that they were studying the post-baccalaureate degree concept, the definition of qualifying CPE and procedures, and definitions relating to experience requirements. Brannon also reported that the National Association of State Boards of Accountancy (NASBA) was meeting in Nashville in June, and the TSCPA Board authorized $1,000 to sponsor a reception at the meeting. Other business included a discussion of an award to honor outstanding accounting educators, but no decision was made on the issue.

Council met in June at the convention in Chattanooga. Claude Blankenship presented the Outstanding Support Award to Paul Royston, of Bristol, in recognition of his exemplary fundraising achievements for the Educational and Memorial Foundation. The EMF had been formed in 1971 and had always struggled for funds throughout its early existence. Royston had served as chair of the EMF for several years and had successfully promoted the value of the foundation, resulting in doubling the size of the Life Associates program.

The June 1985 Board of Directors meeting in Chattanooga addressed basic operational issues, but no long-term action was taken. The Board did approve $150 to provide a refreshment break at a meeting of the newly formed accounting educators group (which would later be named the Tennessee Society of Accounting Educators). The group discussed that the time may have arrived to expand the Society staff role in the planning and execution of the convention.

TSCPA President 1985-86
S. Lawson Crain

S. Lawson Crain, of Jackson, served as president for the 1985-86 Society year. At the September Board of Directors meeting, Ernest Baugh, Chair of the Accounting, Review Services & Auditing Standards Committee, presented the committee's plan to respond to certain FASB exposure drafts. The Board encouraged the committee to proceed with the plan. Lisa McIntosh presented a proposal from the Career Counseling Committee to establish a student membership category that would be available to junior and senior accounting majors at Tennessee colleges and universities. The Board recommended the committee develop written criteria for the category for consideration at the December meeting. At the December Board meeting, the main item of business was the approval of the student membership classification. Also, the formation of the Tennessee Society of Accounting Educators was noted. Council met the next day and approved the student membership category.

On May 9, 1986, the Board of Directors met at the Society office in Nashville. The main issue of discussion focused on the State Board of Accountancy sunset review and developing Society policies with regard to the TSBA. The Directors approved the following actions and position statements:

- There should be no residency restrictions for the issuance of a certificate as a CPA.

- All individual practitioners and firms engaging in the practice of public accounting should be required to register with the State Board of Accountancy.
- The Directors are opposed to the licensing of personal financial planners.
- A consideration of the post-baccalaureate degree was deferred until the May 1987 meeting, and President-elect Claude Blankenship was asked to appoint a committee to study the issue.
- The Directors appointed Mack Browder to present a policy statement on the "two tier" licensing system at the next meeting.
- Claude Blankenship was appointed to present a proposed policy statement on CPE at the next meeting.

TSCPA President 1986-87
Claude E. Blankenship

The June 22, 1986, meeting of the Board was held at the Park Vista Hotel in Gatlinburg, with President Claude Blankenship, of Nashville, presiding. Blankenship reported that the committee to study the post-baccalaureate requirement had been appointed and would report to the Board in May 1987. The Board approved presenting policies 1, 2 and 3 to the Council the next day for approval. In addition, the following policies would be presented as well:
- The CPE requirement of 120 hours in a three-year period should be defined as an average of 40 hours each year, with a minimum of 20 hours each year, and that a specific portion of this requirement be in technical subjects.
- To support the "two tier" system, and that to obtain a license to practice public accounting, the experience requirement should be two years in public practice (or

one year with a master's degree) or three years in state audits or with the Internal Revenue Service.
- To support quality assurance reviews, or a similar practice monitoring system, to be administered by the TSBA.

The next day, Council passed each of the policies with a modification to the CPE requirement. The policy passed by Council stated that CPE should be 80 hours every two years, with a minimum of 20 hours per year.

On Sept. 26, 1986, the Board of Directors heard a report from Dr. Jan Williams, chair of the ad hoc committee on post-baccalaureate education. Other members of the committee were Wynne Baker, Laverne English, Harice Pace, Axel Swang and Robert Sweeney. The committee had researched the topic thoroughly, considered the pros and cons of the proposed requirement, and reached the conclusion that the requirement should be implemented in Tennessee. Florida had passed a similar requirement in 1982, and Tennessee was among the first states to pass the 150-hour education requirement to sit for the CPA exam. A motion to endorse the concept passed unanimously, and the committee was asked to submit a proposed timetable for implementation at the Dec. 5 Board of Directors meeting.

> Tennessee was among the first states to pass the 150-hour education requirement to sit for the CPA exam.

Another long-term issue was also addressed at this meeting. For years, the Society had struggled with the office space problem. Lease vs. buy had been discussed by the Board for several years, with no long-term decision made. Darrel Tongate, on behalf of the Finance Committee, recommended to the Board that $300,000 be restricted for the purpose of acquiring a permanent headquarters. The Board approved a restriction of $250,000.

The next meeting of the Board was on Dec. 5 at the Opryland Hotel. Dr. Jan Williams presented the final implementation plan for the post-baccalaureate requirement. Their recommendation was that individuals qualifying to sit for the CPA exam on or after July 1, 1990, be required to obtain at least 150 semester hours of college education. The Board passed a motion that Council take an affirmative position and accept the proposed implementation plan. The next day, Council met and approved the post-baccalaureate requirement by acclamation. The law was passed by the Tennessee Legislature on April 14, 1987.

In 2014, Dr. Jan Williams recalled his experience and involvement in the implementation of the 150-hour law, saying:

"My memories of the events leading up to the 150-hour requirement in Tennessee are vivid, and I hope accurate. That was a long time ago. My first recollection is a dinner meeting at the Opryland Hotel of the board of TSCPA in about 1985. I was vice president of TSCPA and Claude Blankenship, then with Touche Ross, was president-elect. We were sitting beside each other, and he asked me what he, as president-elect, should be thinking about doing during this year as president that anybody would remember. I mentioned the 150-hour requirement to him for two reasons. First, nationally this had been endorsed as a goal, but the effort was having a hard time getting off the ground, with only three states having gotten on board: Hawaii, Utah and Florida. Of those, only Florida was a real major factor, and if the others didn't move on this fairly soon, my fear was the entire initiative would fail. Second, the Tennessee State Board of Accountancy was up for sunset review the next year, and the accountancy law had to be reconsidered to sustain the profession in Tennessee. My thought was that it would make more sense to make a major change in education requirements as part of a package of other items included in the sunset review, rather than to consider the 150-hour requirement separately in some other year. I also positioned it that Tennessee had the chance to be either early or late in doing this. Early if we went for it the next year; late if we waited six or seven years until the state board was again under sunset review.

"A few days or weeks later, Claude called me and asked me if I would be willing to chair a TSCPA committee to get the ball rolling on the 150-hour requirement. I agreed to do this, and I remember telling him that I thought Axel Swang at Lipscomb was a key to success. I didn't know Axel personally, but knew his reputation and the respect Tennessee CPAs had for him. I thought the combination of Axel (more senior, from a smaller, private school in Middle Tennessee) and myself (at the time younger, from a large state school in East Tennessee) would be a good combination. I scheduled an appointment with Axel at his office at Lipscomb, went there and within a few minutes he was on board. This surprised me, because the word on the street was that smaller schools were resisting the 150-hour requirement out of fear that it would reduce their ability to deliver accounting education, which would become dominated by larger schools with larger faculties, etc.

"Claude put the committee together with myself as chair and Axel, Wynne Baker, Laverne English, Harice Pace and Robert Sweeney as members. We moved it through the TSCPA process, spoke in other forums (state board, Tennessee Society of Accounting Educators, etc.) in Tennessee, and it was passed in relatively short order as part of the sunset review.

"In summary, compared to the other states, the 150-hour requirement passed quickly. It picked up the momentum nationally and placed Tennessee in a leadership position that carried forward for a long time. I and others went all over the place presenting the case, and particularly trying to alleviate the fears of small colleges and the fear that it would create reciprocity problems. I personally went to Georgia, Kentucky, Alabama, North Carolina, South Carolina, Mississippi, Ohio, Rhode Island, Iowa and probably others that I am not thinking of right now. Most of these were at the invitation of state societies that were aware of the Tennessee experience."

At the May 8, 1987, Board meeting, Blankenship asked John Brown, Lawson Crain and Mickey Ison to serve with Michael Collins and James Clift on a committee to search for a permanent office location. The Board also approved the purchase of a modem and other equipment necessary to participate in the AICPA/Dialcom "CPA Link" electronic mailbox.

CHAPTER TWO
1987-1992

The Profession Polices Itself

The June 22, 1987, Council meeting, at the Hyatt Regency Grand Cypress in Orlando, Fla., marked the end of an era. This was the last meeting Nels T. "Ted" Moody would attend as the executive director of TSCPA. He had been in the position since Aug. 21, 1967. Under his leadership, Society membership had grown from 772 to over 4,300 members and staff had increased from one to seven. Moody was recognized at the convention with a rousing standing ovation. Business conducted at the meeting included a report of the Office Search Committee, which had not yet developed any recommendations. Robert Brannon reported on the AICPA spring council meeting. Part of his report included the AICPA Plan to Restructure Professional Standards (known as the Anderson Report). Council voted to encourage all TSCPA members to vote for the restructure.

Two factors had led to the issuance of the Anderson Report (from the AICPA Special Committee on Standards of Professional Conduct for Certified Public Accountants) in October 1986 and the Treadway Commission Report (National Commission on Fraudulent Financial Reporting) in October 1987. First, the savings and loan crisis and other financial scandals of the early 1980s had once again raised Congressional interest in the CPA profession. In February 1985,

Tennessee Governor Ned McWherter officially recognizes the centennial celebration of the CPA profession with a state proclamation. From left are: Pam Baldridge, CPA, of Nashville; Don Royston, CPA, of Kingsport; Governor McWherter; Vicki Dunn, CPA, of Memphis; and Brad Floyd, TSCPA Executive Director.

Rep. John Dingell, Chair of the Subcommittee on Oversight and Investigations of the House Committee on Energy and Commerce, initiated three years of hearings into the profession's self-regulatory system. Second, since the mid-1970s, the Big Eight firms, as well as regional and local firms, were increasingly providing management advisory services for their clients. The "purists" of the profession felt that consulting for audit clients was lessening the independence and objectivity of CPAs. However, the AICPA (and the AICPA-created Public Oversight Board) saw no problem with the practice and did not impose any rules to prohibit it. The Anderson Report called for a peer review system to be implemented and a total revamp of the Code of Professional Conduct. The final report of the Treadway Commission recommended 49 sweeping changes to the governance of the profession.

Art Sparks, of Union City, served on the TSCPA Peer Review Committee for many years and was engaged with the program on a national level as well. He recalls:

"Tennessee CPAs, like most in the U.S., approached the new peer review program with apprehension. While the stated reason for the program was to enhance the quality of work by our profession through self-regulation, one of the reasons was to self-regulate ourselves before the regulators (State Board, GAO, DOL, etc.) began a comprehensive program of their own. The majority knew that it was for the best, but hated to think that someone would be looking over their shoulder at everything they did. The program was approved without many understanding exactly how the system would work, but its purpose was to be educational and remedial, not punitive.

"The program maintains its purpose today, and it has helped the overall quality of the profession and created a self-regulation system like no other profession has. The peer review program has been here for more than 30 years and continues to evolve. While there have been changes in the past, the future appears to hold a complete makeover of the program. Today, the AICPA leadership is in the process of looking at the use of technology to enhance the program and potentially reduce some of the burden on the firm."

The Board of Directors meeting on June 24, 1987, was led by President Don Royston, of Kingsport, with Brad Floyd, assistant executive director, handling the staff duties. The Plan to Restructure Professional Standards was endorsed by the Board, and an implementation committee was to be formed to communicate the plan with the members. Claude Blankenship presented a Building Committee report

TSCPA President 1987-88
C. Don Royston

and discussed the committee's plan to communicate a building purchase proposal to chapters prior to the Dec. 5 interim Council meeting. The Board requested that the committee present a "lease vs. buy" analysis, along with the pros and cons of owning a building, at its next meeting. At the July meeting, Michael Collins presented the

TSCPA past presidents meet with retiring Executive Director Ted Moody during the 1987 TSCPA annual convention in Orlando, Fla. From left are: Joe Kraft, CPA, of Nashville; Bill Sharp, CPA, of Knoxville; Bob Brannon, CPA, of Nashville; Maxie Patton, CPA, of Nashville; Bernie Stone, CPA, of Chattanooga; William Frazee, CPA, of Memphis; Albert Miller Sr., CPA, of Knoxville; Alvah Carrol, CPA, of Memphis; Ted Moody; Lawson Crain, CPA, of Jackson; Mack Browder, CPA, of Memphis; Claude Blankenship, CPA, of Nashville; Herbert Rhea, CPA, of Memphis, John Glenn Jr., CPA, of Nashville; Tom Burgess, CPA, of Nashville; and Paul Bradshaw, CPA, of Chattanooga.

Building Committee report, which called for a lease renewal through March 31, 1990. They also increased the restricted fund balance by $40,000 and renamed the account as a "designated fund."

Brad Floyd assumed the position of TSCPA executive director on Sept. 1, 1987, and he still leads the Society today.

On Sept. 21, 1987, the U.S. Postal Service issued a centennial CPA stamp, and the week of Sept. 20-26 was proclaimed "CPA week" by Gov. Ned McWherter.

Oct. 2, 1987, was the next meeting of the Board of Directors. In his first meeting as the new executive director, Floyd was absent due to the impending birth of his second child. Robert Brannon reported on recent State Board rulemaking activities and AICPA initiatives. The main issue was the ongoing FTC investigation of the ethical prohibition of the acceptance of contingent fees and commissions by CPAs. The AICPA intended to vigorously oppose any attempt by the FTC to change the rules.

The Dec. 4 meeting was highlighted by the formation of a new chapter: Elk Valley. The chapter would be comprised of Coffee, Franklin, Lincoln, Bedford, Marshall and Moore counties. Gary Hunt presented a petition signed by 34 TSCPA members requesting the formation of the chapter, and the request was approved. The Board also voted unanimously to accept a new two-year lease proposal. The Board discussed concerns raised over the level of activity at Council meetings and the overall purpose of Council. It was agreed that although some Council meeting's agendas were longer than others, no recommendations for change would be made now. Council met the next day and approved the Elk Valley Chapter and the building lease proposal.

TSCPA Executive Director
B. Bradford Floyd

Members of the AICPA and TSCPA overwhelmingly voted in favor of the recommendations of the Anderson Report. These included a code of conduct consisting of principles and rules (the basic structure of which is still used to date) and a requirement for a practice-monitoring program for members in public practice. It also mandated CPE, and that by 2000, applicants for AICPA membership would have to acquire 150 college semester hours. TSCPA had been on the leading edge of adopting all of these proposals.

In April 1988, the TSBA passed new rules requiring 80 hours of CPE every two years. The new Code of Professional Conduct of the AICPA was also released that month, and the AICPA approved its first national advertising campaign, themed "The Measure of Excellence." The AICPA Council also approved the FTC agreement concerning commissions and contingent fees.

On May 6, 1988, the Board of Directors met in the TSCPA office. John Brown made a motion, which was approved, to include a $10 contribution check-off for the Tennessee CPA Political Action Committee on the 1989-90 dues invoice. Discussion was held regarding the mandatory quality review for CPA firms, and the Board fully supported TSCPA involvement in administering the program. A resolution was passed to defer enforcement of certain prohibitions in the Code of Ethics relating to contingent fees, commissions, advertising and solicitation, and form of practice and name until the issue was settled at the national level. West Tennessee was in line to host the 1991 convention but opted out. The Board voted to recommend to Council that the convention be a three-day cruise. A motion to delete the provisional member category was passed.

Council met at the Peabody Hotel in Memphis on June 27, 1988. The cruise convention motion was passed, but the Board decision to eliminate the provisional member category was not. The category was retained, and the dues for these members was raised $100. Claude Blankenship announced the creation of the Paul L. Royston Scholarship Fund (Mr. Royston had passed away earlier in the year). A scholarship from this fund would be awarded annually to the top accounting student in the state. Don Royston also introduced Don Hummel, the new administrator of the TSBA.

The Board of Directors met in the Society office on Sept. 23, 1988, with Raymond F. Kamler, of Memphis, serving as Society president. The acceptance of credit cards for CPE courses was approved. The Board agreed that a valid CPA certificate was required for continuation of TSCPA membership except for retired or Life Members. Therefore, members whose licenses were not renewed by the State Board were to be contacted by staff to ascertain their intentions to renew their license. After

TSCPA President 1988-89
Raymond F. Kamler

reviewing the comments from the previous Leadership Conference, the Board's consensus was to hold future conferences in one full day (CPE in the morning, followed by a joint luncheon and committee meetings in the afternoon).

> The Board endorsed the Accountancy Act and voted to take all reasonable steps to secure enactment. It passed the legislature with little opposition and was signed into law by Gov. Ned McWherter on May 29, 1989.

The office space issue dominated the Board and Council meetings held Dec. 2-3 at the Opryland Hotel. Michael Collins, Chair of the Long-Range Planning Committee, provided pictures of the recommended building for purchase (3 Churchill Place) and the best lease alternative (the Financial Plaza Building). The Board voted to recommend to Council that leasing was the best option at this time. At the Council meeting, several motions were made, withdrawn and tabled with respect to the building issue. Finally, a motion to direct the Board of Directors and the Long-Range Planning Committee to consider the options of buying a building or leasing a building and report their findings to Council was passed. Council also approved a recommendation to lease space in the Financial Plaza Building, at 200 Powell Place in Brentwood, for the next five years. In addition, the Board voted that fellow members must maintain a valid CPA certificate to remain a member in TSCPA, and a motion to oppose a NASBA registry of CPE sponsors was passed by the Board.

The Board of Directors met by conference call on Jan. 3, 1989, to finalize the details of the office relocation. On April 1, the Society office was relocated, and the first Board of Directors meeting in the new office was held May 5, 1989. Executive Director Brad Floyd reported to the Board that the move had been completed on time and within budget. The new Accountancy Act was expected to be passed by the Tennessee General Assembly during the 1989 session. The new act called for all fees collected by the TSBA to be deposited into a special fund for operating costs; thus, the state's general fund would no longer be able to use any of the operating funds or be liable for operating expenses. This new funding method was expected to give the TSBA additional independence and resources in order to more effectively regulate and enforce the accountancy law. Another significant effect of the new law was to phase out continued licensure of public accountants in Tennessee.

The state legislature's actions to make public accountants (PAs) a "dying class" of licensees was a very controversial action among both CPAs and PAs in Tennessee. TSCPA leaders realized the urgent need to quickly eliminate future licensure of PAs when an increasing number of potential CPA candidates began applying to sit for the PA exam as a result of the newly increased educational requirement to sit for the CPA exam in Tennessee. The amendment to implement the 150-hour requirement would become effective on April 4, 1993, making Tennessee the fourth state in the nation to embrace the higher educational requirement.

Under the old law, PAs had been licensed to perform the same attest services that CPAs were licensed to perform; however, PAs were not required to complete the higher education experience or examination requirements equivalent to CPAs. Under the leadership of TSCPA Legislation Committee Chair Will Pugh and Sen. Ben Atchley of Knoxville, the Society hammered out a deal with the Tennessee Association of PAs to stop licensing any further PAs, in exchange for granting CPA certificates to a limited number of existing PAs who had been licensed for at least 20 years or met the significantly higher experience and educational requirements spelled out in the new law.

The legislation passed to make PAs a dying class in 1989. Although it was controversial at the time, it proved to be a successful way to eliminate future licensure of PAs. Licensing two different classes of accountants had been confusing to the public, and this provision of the new Accountancy Act was necessary to ease that confusion and strengthen the CPA profession in Tennessee. The amendment also removed the PA representatives on the Tennessee State Board of Accountancy and established a three-year term limit for state board members. The new law called for the state board to consist of nine CPAs, one attorney and one public member.

Will Pugh would go on to lead TSCPA initiatives to successfully amend the Tennessee Accountancy Law multiple times over the next two decades. Thanks to his leadership, Tennessee established itself as a leader among the states in pursuit of uniform accountancy laws and rules.

The Board endorsed the act and voted to take all reasonable steps to secure enactment. The Accountancy Act passed the legislature with little opposition and was signed into law by Gov. Ned McWherter on May 29, 1989.

TSCPA President 1989-90
Grady P. Williams

The Board also passed a motion to participate in the Joint Ethics Enforcement Program of the AICPA. Grady Williams, President-elect, asked the Board to consider a two-day retreat during one quarterly meeting, and the Board concurred that September would be an appropriate time. Kamler proposed that a requested contribution to the EMF be added to the dues invoice, but the Board did not approve the idea. A motion to reimburse Board members' travel expenses up to $200 to attend the convention was approved.

Starting with the May 1989 issue, the TSCPA publication was renamed the *Tennessee CPA, Journal of the Tennessee Society of Certified Public Accountants* and was reformatted. The May edition featured a front cover with a photograph, and the *Journal* featured a more magazine-like appearance. Also, more articles from outside authors were included, and the publication was made available to public libraries for the first time.

The Council met on June 29, 1989, at the Opryland Hotel in Nashville. The Board met on Sept. 15 at the Society office, with Grady Williams, of Chattanooga, assuming the role of president. Jack Kennedy, a member of the AICPA Implementation Committee for the Plan to Restructure Professional Standards, was present at the meeting. He presented a request on behalf of the AICPA that the Board endorse the proposal to require firms that audit public companies to join the AICPA's SEC Practice Section. A motion was passed by the Board to support this recommendation. David Curbo, Chair of the TSCPA Quality Review Committee, updated the Board on the status of the program. He requested the approval of a consulting agreement with Thomas Burgess to provide the technical consulting services for the Quality Review Program in Tennessee. The Board approved the proposal and authorized the committee to invoice firms enrolled in the program during December 1989 for annual administration fees.

Personal financial planning had emerged as a growth area for CPAs. The new Accountancy Act had included a provision that nothing in the law prohibited CPAs from engaging in this activity. The issue of state licensing of financial planners had been opposed by the Board years earlier. At the Dec. 1, 1989, board meeting, a Legislation Committee proposal to modify this position was presented. The Board recognized the committee's need to be flexible on this issue and possibly support a compromise that would minimize adverse effects on the accounting profession. The Board also passed a recommendation that non-members (or those not employed by a Tennessee CPA firm) be charged an additional $25 per CPE program.

The Council meeting on Dec. 2, 1989, was held at the Opryland Hotel. Council re-affirmed the Society's policy of opposing the licensing of personal financial planners, but it authorized the Legislation Committee to support compromise legislation if necessary. Maxie Patton presented an activity report of the TSBA and announced the TSBA was establishing a mandatory Positive Enforcement Program and would exempt Tennessee CPA firms completing the TSCPA Quality Review program.

An article in the January 1990 *Tennessee CPA Journal* presented the operational statistics of a national MAP survey of CPA firms. The non-national, multi-owner firms were broken into three categories. Small firms were defined as those with less than $350,000 in revenue, medium firms had revenue between $350,000 and $900,000, and large firms had over $900,000 in revenue. Net income annually per owner of small Tennessee CPA firms was $35,794. For the medium firms, this figure was $73,695. Large firms' annual net income per owner was $88,556. Salaries in Tennessee were lower than the national average. Professional-supervisors and managers were paid an average of $34,491 per year. Professional-seniors with 4-5 years of experience earned $26,940, while staff with 0-3 years of experience averaged a salary of $19,192. The average partner billing rate of all CPA firms in Tennessee was $77.05 per hour.

In January 1990, TSCPA surpassed the 5,000-member mark. A three-minute radio spot (TN CPA Today Radio) advocating CPAs was being broadcasted weekly in 13 markets around the state. Steven Curtis Chapman provided the music for the ad. By that time, 13 states had passed the 150-hour requirement, and 16 more had introduced the bill in their respective legislatures. The AICPA had enacted CPE requirements for members that included 60 hours every three years at first, then increasing to 120 hours per three-year period afterward.

> In January 1990, TSCPA surpassed the 5,000-member mark.

May 4, 1990, was the next meeting of the Board. The Board discussed specific legislation that had been passed concerning a prohibition on acceptance of commissions and contingent fees for CPAs in public practice. Maxie Patton, TSBA Chair, stated that Governor McWherter desired to appoint new board members prior to the end of May and requested that TSCPA submit a list of qualified CPAs. In a straw vote, the Board unanimously opposed an AICPA proposal to admit non-CPAs as members. John Brown recommended the Board consider loaning the Society's designated building fund (now totaling $330,000) interest-free to the Educational and Memorial Foundation. No action was taken on this recommendation. Brown also asked that Don Hummel, executive director of the TSBA, be approved as an honorary member of TSCPA. The Board accepted this proposition favorably, and deferred to Council to act upon it.

Council met in June at the Holiday Inn World's Fair Park in Knoxville. Jan Williams, Chair of the Relations with Educational Institutions Committee and a member of the AICPA 150-hour Implementation Committee, presented an update on the implementation of the proposal and summarized certain changes in the Tennessee Accountancy Law that would be needed to conform with the AICPA proposal. John Brown moved that Don Hummel be admitted as an honorary member, and the motion passed. Brown also made a motion that the Society loan the designated fund to the EMF secured by a non-interest-bearing note, payable not less than six months after demand. The motion was seconded, discussed and tabled.

TSCPA President 1990-91
Darrel E. Tongate

On June 27, 1990, the Board of Directors was called to order by President Darrel Tongate, of Nashville. Don Royston presented information about the 1991 Cruise Convention. Tongate appointed Casey Stuart, John Brown, Frank Greer and Charles Young to a committee to recommend future use of the designated fund.

On Sept. 21, 1990, the Board met at the Society office in Brentwood. Tom Burgess, technical consultant for the AICPA/TSCPA Quality Review Program, reported that of the 87 reviews scheduled for completion during the year, 19 had been completed and accepted by the committee. The Board recommended that

TSCPA Council policies be amended to allow for the automatic termination of Council membership of members who missed two consecutive meetings. A letter requesting Board endorsement of a Cleveland-area chapter was considered. The Board recommended that the chapter not be formed at this time due to the limited number of CPAs in the area and the close proximity of the Chattanooga and Knoxville chapters.

The major item of business dealt with the Educational and Memorial Foundation. The EMF was finally building the fund to a level that could support the annual scholarships. Total fund balance on March 31, 1983, had been $94,082. Through the efforts of many individuals, including a plea to all Council members from Scholarship Committee Chair David Lynn Jr., the structure of the EMF with regard to TSCPA had been raised in 1986. This included a recommendation from PricewaterhouseCoopers to qualify the Foundation as a 509(a)(3) organization, but no action had been taken at that time. Chuck Dennard presented a report completed by Arthur Andersen at the request of TSCPA that recommended the Society move the CPE program to the EMF 501(c)(3) entity and away from the Society's 501(c)(6) organization. A motion to transfer the program was passed that included provisions requiring that the president and executive director be empowered to negotiate and execute an appropriate contractual arrangement between the two groups, that the activity must be revenue-neutral, and that the foundation's Board of Trustees be expanded to include the Society's Board of Directors.

The next Board of Directors meeting was held Nov. 30, 1990, at the Opryland Hotel. Casey Stuart, Chair of the Society's Designated Fund Balance Committee, made the following motions, which were passed unanimously:
- The Board recommend that Council adopt a policy of making an annual contribution to the EMF equal to the greater of $2 per member as of the end of the year, or the

excess of revenue over expenses not to exceed an annual amount of $30,000.
- The Board recommend to Council to remove the term "designated" from the fund balance, and that the $330,000 become unrestricted.
- The Board recommend to Council that the annual budget include a projected unrestricted fund balance not less than the amount equal to member dues collected for the most recent year.

Discussion of creating an associate member classification followed, and John Brown was instructed to work with the Bylaws Committee to establish the classification. The Board also passed a motion to recommend to the TSCPA Educational and Memorial Foundation Board of Trustees that the CPE program be transferred to the foundation. Council met on Dec. 1, 1990, and recommendations from the Designated Fund Balance Committee were passed and other normal business matters were approved.

U.S. Sen. Jim Sasser confers with Doug Smith, CPA, TSCPA Legislation Committee Chair, during a meeting in Washington, D.C.

The May Board of Directors meeting featured an announcement that the Tennessee Legislature had passed a TSCPA-sponsored bill that would change the educational requirement in the Accountancy Law to 150 semester hours, as opposed to a baccalaureate degree plus 30 hours. Also, the bill changed the requirement so that the education must be acquired before sitting for the CPA exam rather than "no later than 90 days after sitting." Will Pugh made a motion, which was passed unanimously, that the Board support the CPE Support Services Agreement between TSCPA and EMF. The associate member classification for persons who had completed the requirements to be eligible to sit for the CPA exam and were employed by a member of TSCPA was approved.

> President Darrel Tongate presented a report on behalf of the EMF, announcing that the foundation had fully assumed the responsibility of operating the CPE program.

Council met on June 27, 1991, on the *Fantasy* cruise ship in the Bahamas. The bylaws proposal to create the associate member category was considered, and Council approved a mail ballot to all members to vote on the change. Maxie Patton of the TSBA reported that of the 137 completed Quality Reviews in the current year, 28 percent were rated "acceptable," 35 percent were rated "moderately deficient," and 36 percent were rated "seriously deficient." President Darrel Tongate presented a report on behalf of the EMF, announced that the foundation had fully assumed the responsibility of operating the CPE program, and reported that the Support Services Agreement had been approved.

Tongate later commented that he considered stopping or avoiding any legislation that would have had an adverse effect on the profession at the time, such as a sales tax on services or reducing the effectiveness of the State Board of Accountancy, as significant milestones during his tenure as president. Tongate said, "I followed

Grady Williams as president and I was followed by Will Pugh, probably two of the most influential men I knew at the time other than Joe Kraft, my mentor and great friend." Tongate considered himself a "small part of the group of members who in my opinion were the bedrock of the Society at that time" and who did "everything in their power to keep the profession on solid ground and in control of its own destiny." Tongate served four years as Society treasurer before becoming president, and in that role he worked with Wanda Jones, TSCPA's finance director, to set up the Society's in-house accounting system. He would later serve as executive director of the State Board of Accountancy, which "helped keep the two entities close instead of allowing a gap to occur." Tongate felt "especially blessed to serve with some of the greatest minds and personalities our profession has ever known."

TSCPA President 1991-92
Will J. Pugh

Will Pugh, of Knoxville, served as president for 1991-92. The first meeting of the Board of Directors was held on Sept. 20. The Board endorsed the AICPA amendments to Rule 505 (Form of Practice and Name) and Rule 301 (Confidential Client Information) to the Code of Professional Conduct. The bylaws amendment ballot to create the associate member class was delayed until Council could consider some changes in the language of the proposal. The Board voted to adopt a policy that the convention be held out of state every other year. Pugh appointed a committee comprised of Darrel Tongate, William "Billy" Griesbeck and Bobby Meadows to make recommendations regarding a policy on chapter-sponsored CPE, which might be in competition with the state CPE schedule.

At the Dec. 5, 1991, Board meeting, Grady Williams requested the Board to reconsider the policy established in 1990 regarding the requirement that the proposed budget each year project an unrestricted fund balance not less than the amount equal to member dues collected for the most recent year. The Board voted to recommend to Council that the policy be changed to read, "The annual budget presented to Council for adoption will recognize the expenses, financial needs and future capital requirements when setting the annual budget. An unrestricted fund balance shall be maintained to cover a major portion of one year's projected operating and capital expenditures." The Board discussed the philosophy of enacting smaller increases in dues more frequently, rather than larger increases occurring every five to seven years. The motion to approve was passed, and dues were increased $5 for the next year.

President-elect Billy Griesbeck, of Memphis, proposed that a two-day Board "workshop" be held in September 1992. This would allow the Board to devote more time to strategic planning and professional issues. Board members agreed that a workshop would be useful and that, since it was to be a working meeting, Board members should attend without spouses. This would be the first extended workshop meeting of the Board, a tradition that continues today.

The Board discussed the Society's prior support of the Tennessee Federal Tax Institute, Inc., and noted that TSCPA should not be restricted from hosting a high-quality federal tax conference of its own each year. A motion was passed to repeal the Council policy in support of the TFTI.

The Board also approved a proposal to provide guidelines on "valuable service" when selecting chapter nominees for Life Member status. A motion was passed that stated members who have reached age 62 should complete the following service requirement prior to being nominated for Life Member. These requirements were:
- After 20 years: actively served on chapter or state board and as a member of a state committee.
- After 25 years: must have actively served on Council and as a member of a state committee.
- After 30 years: must have actively served as a member on a chapter or state committee.
- After 40 years: automatic.

The Board reviewed a proposal to retain Dan Elrod as TSCPA's legislative counsel and registered lobbyist. They also discussed the continued utilization of Doug Smith as legislative consultant. After discussion, the Board approved a motion to continue the current agreement with Smith for one more year in order to facilitate an orderly transition, and Elrod would become the Society's outside lobbyist thereafter. A motion to offer a one-year complimentary membership to successful CPA candidates was passed unanimously.

At the Dec. 7, 1991, Council meeting, the associate member classification was passed. The most pressing business presented to Council involved CPE. Chapters had been asking for clarification about the rules governing their CPE given the new TSCPA and EMF agreement. A motion was passed that encouraged chapters to provide CPE, with the condition that the program should not exceed four hours per day and should not be scheduled to conflict with CPE courses offered by the foundation. All CPE courses must meet TSBA requirements, and detailed records of the CPE must be kept. The Board motion to repeal Council policy in support of the Tennessee Federal Tax Institute, Inc., was not passed by Council but was supplanted by a motion that the Society shall cooperate with the Institute.

> A motion to offer a one-year complimentary membership to successful CPA candidates was passed unanimously.

John Brown proposed an "inactive" member category for those members who have temporarily left the workforce for military duty, disability or domestic responsibilities. The motion passed. Also passed was the Board motion concerning the annual budget and the unrestricted fund balance issue. Ted Moody was elected an honorary TSCPA member. A motion to hold the convention out of state every other year failed to be passed by Council.

President Pugh requested Board members consider a proposal made by Jim Shelby regarding the Investment Committee at the May 1992 Board meeting. After discussion of the proposal, a motion was passed to expand the committee to five members, four of whom would be appointed by the president, with the treasurer serving as an ex-officio member. Pugh discussed the advantage of having staggered biennial CPE reporting, whereby half of the CPA certificates would be renewed each year. A motion to recommend this proposal to the TSBA was passed. Pugh announced the membership had approved the bylaws amendment concerning the associate member category. Darrel Tongate made a motion, which was passed, that complimentary membership for successful candidates include state and chapter fees unless otherwise instructed by any chapter.

The regular Council meeting convened at the Glenstone Lodge in Gatlinburg on June 22, 1992. Council approved a contribution to the EMF of $11,072 (5,536 members times $2 per member). Singleton Wolfe, of Knoxville, was elected an honorary member.

The Board of Directors held its first Workshop on Aug. 27-29 at Fairfield Glade. President Billy Griesbeck presided. The Board discussed future conventions and made several recommendations, including that organized recreation and the children's program should be a priority when selecting a location and that conventions should be held within a one-day drive. The Board requested more chapter events be covered in the *Tennessee CPA Journal*, and that more Tennessee news rather than national news be included in the publication. The detailed structure of the Investment Committee was approved. A motion was passed to extend the consulting agreement with Doug Smith as a legislative consultant for three more months and then pay him a severance payment of $3,600. Ways to recruit

TSCPA President 1992-93
William G. Griesbeck

and retain members were discussed. The Board recommended that the terms of committee chairs be limited to three years and the terms of committee members to six years. Finally, a motion was passed that instructed the Strategic Planning Committee to provide the Board with an analysis concerning the lease vs. buy issue regarding Society headquarters.

The next Board meeting was held Nov. 20, 1992, at the Society office. Brad Floyd and Charles Dennard reviewed current issues in the 1993 legislative session. These included a proposal to establish LLCs in Tennessee, a sunset review of the accountancy board, tort reform proposals and a proposal to extend the sales tax to professional services. Floyd discussed the possibility of co-hosting annual conventions with other state CPA societies. North Carolina and South Carolina had expressed an interest in doing so in 1996 in Nashville. Staff was instructed to continue discussions with these organizations. Floyd updated the Board on the progress of the Strategic Planning Committee concerning permanent office space. The committee would ask Council to express its view on the lease vs. buy issue.

> Council voted 54-46 to direct the president to appoint an Office Facilities Committee to consider new office space options.

The interim Council meeting was held at the Opryland Hotel in December. The budget was passed without a dues increase. Following a discussion, Council voted 54-46 to direct the president to appoint an Office Facilities Committee to consider new office space options. Ray Butler Sr., of Memphis, made a motion that was duly seconded to instruct the Council and the Legislation Committee to actively seek the repeal of the Professional Privilege Tax ($200 per year), which had been enacted in April 1992 by the Tennessee Legislature. The motion failed.

David Curbo presented an update on the Quality Review Program, which was renamed the Peer Review Program in 1994. Since its inception in 1989, 80 percent of reports had been unmodified, 18 percent modified and 2 percent adverse. The firms receiving modified and adverse reports had been issued specific remedial actions that were to be completed in order to remain in the program.

Curbo recalled, "As the peer review program was fleshed out, one of the selling points was that by instituting a robust self-regulation program through peer review, we could maintain control of our industry instead of having the equivalent of the IRS regulating the audit industry. It was also presented that the peer review would be 'confidential, educational and non-punitive.' The Tennessee law as drafted created a 'brick wall' between the peer review program and the board of accountancy so that the board could not know or use the results of a firm's peer review in disciplinary action against the firm, except that the firm was or was not appropriately participating in the peer review program. Appropriate participation in the peer review program would be a condition for maintaining a firm's license, so that was crucial, but other complaints could not be based or buttressed by peer review results. Secondly, the peer review was to be focused on helping the firms do a better job of performing quality reporting engagements, not just identifying mistakes the firm made. Thus, the peer reviews should be systemically focused and not just report a list of errors found. And lastly, the peer reviews should be non-punitive. Firms and individuals would not be punished for the results of their peer reviews as long as they took corrective actions for the mistakes found. Also, the only punishment that could be levied on a firm would be to terminate them from the program. This action would only be taken if the firm failed to take reasonable corrective action or failed to participate in the program."

In a decade and a half, TSCPA had grown not only in membership but also in its leadership and professional development. The activities undertaken in this time period laid the foundation for the professional environment in which Tennessee CPAs operate today.

CHAPTER THREE
1993-1996

Building For the Future

The Office Facilities Committee met on Feb. 6, 1993. Members of the committee were Bob Brannon, Charles Dennard, Marie Dubke and David Frizzell. Discussion was held about the options for the Society's headquarters. All suitable ownership options were limited to build-to-suit proposals. The economic advantages of building vs. leasing over the short and long term were discussed. It was determined that TSCPA would gain an economic advantage over the short term (six years) by leasing office space.

At the April 30, 1993, Board meeting, the Board voted to oppose the AICPA proposal to establish specialty designations, but it did not take a position on the non-CPA ownership of CPA firms as presented by the AICPA. The main item of business dealt with the office space issue. The Board voted to establish an Office Facilities Negotiating Subcommittee to negotiate a six-year lease in the Brentwood area. They also empowered the group to pursue the possibility of acquiring a parcel of land in Brentwood on which to build an office building.

Council met at the Chattanooga Choo-Choo Holiday Inn on June 21. Bob Brannon made a motion to empower the Negotiating Subcommittee to negotiate an office lease of up to five years in the Brentwood area. The motion passed unanimously. Brannon then motioned to also empower the subcommittee to negotiate the purchase of the parcel of land at the corner of Maryland Way and Powell Place in Brentwood. Following a lengthy discussion, the motion was passed by a majority vote.

TSCPA President 1993-94
Joe A. Thorne

The 1993 Board of Directors Workshop was held once again in August at Fairfield Glade. Joe Thorne, of Cookeville, had become Society president. Brad Floyd reported that TSCPA had executed a contract with First American Bank for the purchase of 2.18 acres in Maryland Farms for approximately $380,000. Floyd requested the Board to sign a resolution, recommended by TSCPA attorney Jack Robinson, to approve the purchase of the property. Chuck Dennard made a motion to approve the resolution, and it was passed unanimously. Floyd also reported that a three-year lease renewal at the present office location had been negotiated. The Board unanimously authorized Floyd to sign the renewal. The Professional Ethics Committee had requested the Bylaws Committee change the bylaws to increase its membership from six to eight to allow each chapter to have a representative on the committee. The possibility of offering CPE for reading the *Journal* was approved on a trial basis. President Thorne presented a letter from the Tennessee Accounting Hall of Fame, which had requested TSCPA to co-sponsor the 1993 Hall of Fame. The Board approved up to $1,000 be contributed, contingent upon additional information being obtained and subsequent presidential approval.

A business item with a long-lasting impact was presented by Mike Shmerling. He presented a request from the Nashville Chapter that the Board reconsider the current officer rotation plan. For years, the Board had approved the state officer positions by chapter, with each chapter having an established timeframe for each of the officer positions. The Nashville Chapter's concern with the current system was to allow more representation from the larger chapters in the Society officer positions. Thorne was requested to appoint a subcommittee to study the current organization structure and recommend to the Board ways to properly address the Nashville Chapter's concerns.

> In 1993, TSCPA executed a contract with First American Bank for the purchase of 2.18 acres in the Maryland Farms office park in Brentwood.

In September 1993, David Costello became the director of the Tennessee State Board of Accountancy.

In November, the Board met at the Society office. Pervis Ballew made a motion that the Board endorse a proposal to obtain Council authorization to proceed with the development of building plans for a headquarters building. The motion passed unanimously. In light of the financial need of building, a motion was passed to recommend to Council that the unrestricted fund balance policy be amended to read, "A balance shall be maintained to cover a portion of one year's projected operating and capital expenditures" (the word "major" was removed from the existing policy). The motion passed unanimously.

The interim Council meeting was held at the Loews Vanderbilt Plaza on Dec. 4. Council approved the restatement of the unrestricted fund policy. They also authorized the president to appoint an ad hoc building committee to develop construction plans for a headquarters building and to determine the most favorable methods of financing. Council further approved the committee to incur necessary expenses to complete the plans and to present these plans at the June 1994 Council meeting. After years of discussion, TSCPA was finally reaching a consensus on the office space issue.

The TSCPA Organization and Structure Task Force, appointed by President Joe Thorne in reaction to the Nashville Chapter's officer concerns, met on Dec. 17, 1993. Members present were Lawson

Crain, David Frizzell, Billy Griesbeck, David Morgan, Danny Pressley and Joe Thorne. The task force members had reviewed the current policies, and several changes were discussed, including that the officers be elected by the Board of Directors, that the officers be selected from each grand division of the state, and that smaller chapters would group together to allow them to jointly recommend officers. The task force voted to recommend that the Nominating Committee not be required to strictly adhere to an "officer rotation plan," but that it only had to follow TSCPA bylaws that require the committee to solicit and consider officer nominee recommendations by the chapters. While no simple formula existed for selecting officer nominees, the Nominating Committee should consider chapter size, geographic location and other intangibles when selecting future officer nominees.

The task force also discussed the current roles of the Board and Council and considered whether the size and responsibilities of those bodies be changed. They did not provide any specific recommendations but concluded that the current size of Council restricted its ability to effectively serve as a responsive and efficient governing body. It was recommended that Council be expected to serve more of an advisory role and that the Board of Directors continue to act as the day-to-day governing body.

The next meeting of the Board was held on May 6, 1994. Self-study CPE for reading the *Journal* was going well, and the Board voted to continue the program and re-evaluate it in May 1995. Bob Brannon, Chair of the ad hoc Building Committee, presented the preliminary drawings for the new TSCPA headquarters. Casey Stuart presented a report from the Organization and Structure Task Force, and the Board agreed with their recommendations. The Limited Liability Companies Act had been passed by the Tennessee Legislature. After the sunset review, the Accountancy Board had been renewed through June 30, 2002. A proposal from the Personnel Committee to renew the employment contract of Floyd was approved.

Several changes had been implemented with regard to the CPA exam in May 1994. Candidates were now allowed to use calculators, the exam would be held on two days (previously the exam was 2 ½ days), the first Wednesday and Thursday in May and November, and the sections were modified by eliminating Accounting Theory. Also in May, the TSBA changed the CPE requirements (effective July 1, 1994) to require certificate holders to earn 60 hours every two years. Persons holding a CPA permit to practice under the "two tier" system were still required to earn 80 hours every two years. Retired or disabled CPAs, as well as those who served in the military, would be exempt from these requirements.

> Several changes were implemented to the CPA exam in May 1994. Candidates were now allowed to use calculators, the exam would be held on two days and the sections were modified by eliminating Accounting Theory.

Council was held at the Marriott's Bay Point Resort in Panama City, Fla., on June 27, 1994. President Joe Thorne called the meeting to order. Council approved a motion that empowered the Society officers to approve documents necessary for construction and financing the headquarters. The Board met briefly on June 29, with Charles Dennard, of Nashville, assuming the role of president.

Fairfield Glade was the location for the Aug. 18-20 Board Workshop. The building project update was presented. The Board requested the Scholarship Committee chair look into new ways of selecting recipients. It was

TSCPA President 1994-95
Charles N. Dennard

recommended by the Board that the committee investigate using an outside professional service in the process. The Board discussed several reasons why educators were not more involved in TSCPA. Phyllis Driver agreed to conduct a random survey of educators and report the results in November.

In September, Dr. Jan Williams was awarded the first annual TSCPA Outstanding Educator Award. His name was again placed in nomination for the AICPA Educator Award for the next year, and he won the award that year as well.

The TSCPA Nominating Committee met on Sept. 30, 1994, at the TSCPA office in Brentwood. Committee Chair Joe Thorne opened the meeting by reviewing the committee's responsibilities as identified in the new bylaws amendment. The committee determined that members should serve longer than one-year terms in order to provide more continuity within the group. A motion was approved to recommend to the Board of Directors that TSCPA bylaws be amended to establish three-year staggered terms for future committee members. Following a lengthy discussion, the

Building Committee members Robert C. Brannon, CPA, and David K. Morgan, CPA, on the future site of the TSCPA headquarters building in Brentwood.

committee decided not to select officer nominees based solely on the chapter rotation plan. Officer selection would be made from a list of qualified candidates submitted by the chapters. Chapter affiliation, leadership qualities and other intangibles would be considered when selecting future officers. The Society staff was instructed to develop a nominating form that would assist the chapters in identifying members to submit as possible officers.

At the November 1994 meeting, Dan Elrod was introduced as the new outside TSCPA lobbyist. President Dennard and Brad Floyd updated the Board on a lawsuit filed by IDS in Federal Court against the Florida Board of Accountancy. The lawsuit was seeking to overturn and invalidate the "holding out" component of the practice of public accounting. The TSCPA Board voted to approve a 50-cent-per-member contribution to the Florida Institute of CPAs in defense of this lawsuit. A settlement was eventually reached. Floyd updated the Board on a request TSCPA had received from the Tennessee State Board of Accountancy to submit a proposal on administering the TSBA Quality Review Program.

Given the recommendations of the Organization and Structure Task Force, the structure of the Nominating Committee was discussed. A motion to amend the bylaws to allow three-year staggered terms for committee members and to allow for the three most recent past presidents to serve on the committee was passed. That motion was then amended to allow past presidents to serve in a non-voting capacity following the year they had served as chair. Dennard updated the Board on the building project. A motion was passed by a majority vote to request that Council approve a $15-per-year (for up to four years) special dues assessment of the membership in order to front-end the cash flow to fund the building.

The interim Council meeting was held on Dec. 3, 1994, at the Opryland Hotel. Society President Dennard called the meeting to order. Joe Thorne, Chair of the Nominating Committee, presented the Board's proposal to change the structure of the committee. The Board's motion to have past presidents serve as non-voting

The new TSCPA headquarters in Brentwood is seen here under construction in 1995-1996.

members of the committee was amended by Council to state that the past three presidents would have voting rights. The immediate past president would serve as the committee chair. The amended motion passed by a majority vote. A ballot to amend the bylaws would be included in the January issue of the *Tennessee CPA Journal*. Thorne also reported that the committee would solicit officer nominations from all chapters and that the method of selecting officers would not follow the "chapter rotation plan." A motion was made to ask the Nominating Committee to seriously consider using the rotation plan in its consideration of officers for 1995-96. The motion failed for lack of a majority vote. The motion to change the composition of the Professional Ethics Committee to allow each chapter to have a member passed unanimously.

President Dennard presented an update on the headquarters construction project. On behalf of the Board of Directors, a motion was made to provide standby authority to the Board to enact a special dues assessment of $15 per year for up to four years to fund the building. The motion was passed by Council. Will Pugh updated the Council on the TSBA activities and introduced Darrel Tongate as the new executive director of TSBA.

The Board of Directors held a conference call on Feb. 28, 1995, to be updated on the building project. Dennard and Floyd stated that space requirements had been reduced by 800 square feet, and the adjusted total cost of the building would be $1,374,083. Bobby Meadows moved, and Ed Lansford seconded, a motion that a $15 dues special assessment be added to the 1995-96 dues invoice. The motion passed. The Board discussed whether a member would forfeit membership if they "marked out" the assessment, and it was decided the member would forfeit membership for non-payment of dues.

On May 5, 1995, the Board met at the Society office. The primary agenda item was a building update. Projected schedules and timelines were discussed, as well as financing options. Dennard asked the Board to adopt a resolution to allow the president and/or executive director to sign financial and construction documents on behalf of the Board. The motion passed unanimously. On a separate motion, which was also passed unanimously, the Board authorized the president to terminate the lease at the current headquarters at the appropriate time to facilitate an orderly transition into the new building. In other news, the Board approved continuing the self-study CPE for reading the *Journal*.

Brad Floyd updated the Board on legislative issues. He reported that Gov. Don Sundquist's administration intended to use reserve funds from state agencies to balance the state budget the following year and that the TSBA would be losing much of its reserve fund. A proposal by the TSBA to separate itself from the Division of Regulatory Boards to become an independent agency was also discussed. The Limited Liability Partnership Act had been passed, which allowed CPA firms an additional option for organization. Dennard reported that the bylaws amendments regarding the Nominating Committee and the Professional Ethics Committee had been passed by vote of the membership. The Board was updated with the news that the Young CPA Committee had put together a statewide CPA softball tournament to be held in Nashville on July 22-23.

Council met at the Peabody Hotel in Memphis on June 26, 1995. Bob Brannon updated the members on the building progress. President Dennard presented the 1995 President's Award to Tom Burgess, of Nashville. Committee reports were reviewed, Grady Williams presented an AICPA update, and a report on the activities of the TSBA was presented by Will Pugh.

TSCPA President 1995-96
Casey M. Stuart

The next meeting of the Board was held Aug. 24-25 at Fairfield Glade. Casey Stuart, of Chattanooga, the president for 1995-96, presided. Stuart updated the Board about a new AIPCA image enhancement program ("Never Underestimate the Value"), which was projected to cost the AICPA a total of $3 million. The Board had a positive reaction to the program and noted it should be supported in some way by TSCPA. Pervis Bellew and Sandra Zehntner reported that the 1995 TSCPA Convention in Memphis resulted in a deficit of $6,500, primarily due to the lower registration fee for first-time attendees. The Board agreed that the Society should encourage first-time attendees at the convention and voted to cover the deficit for the chapter.

The Board reviewed a letter from attorney G. Michael Yopp regarding the discussion to loan TSCPA funds to the Educational and Memorial Foundation. The Board concluded that such a loan should not be allowed. Floyd provided a building update and noted that First American National Bank had approved a construction loan for $1.3 million. He also noted that initial construction bids were higher than anticipated, resulting in revisions to the original design. The Building Committee had selected the Carden Company to construct the building at a cost of $1,250,324. Former President Dennard expressed concern that the building would not be a good investment decision and that it may not be prudent for the Board to move ahead with the construction. The Board concluded that the building was for long-term use and should not be viewed as an investment, and a motion to continue the project was passed unanimously.

Brad Floyd reviewed the work of the AICPA Special Committee on Regulation and Structure of the Profession. The objectives of this committee were to review the current state-based system of regulation and develop recommendations for the AICPA Board that may include a national certification process. New TSBA rules for the experience requirement were covered. The major change in this new requirement affected CPAs not working in public accounting. Three years' experience in government or industry under the direct supervision of a CPA with an active permit would be required in the future. A master's degree with a major or concentration in accounting would count as one year of experience.

The Board considered a request from the Texas Society of CPAs to assist in covering the expense of a lawsuit they had filed against

American Express Tax and Business Services. The Texas Society alleged that American Express had been practicing public accounting without registering with the Texas State Board. If the lawsuit were to be successful, it would likely strengthen the ability of all state boards to regulate these types of entities in their respective states. A motion was passed by the Board of Directors to make a pledge of $3,000 to assist in this endeavor. The Court eventually issued a permanent injunction barring American Express from issuing financial statements under reports that assert any expertise in accounting.

The Board met on Nov. 17, 1995, in the Brentwood office. President Casey Stuart recommended the Board amend the current budget to provide funding for acquisition of appropriate phone and computer systems, as well as furnishings for the new building. A motion to approve $160,000 was passed by a majority vote. Floyd updated the group on the building progress. Ground-breaking and construction

TSCPA Headquarters Ribbon-Cutting Ceremony, June 1996. Pictured left to right are: Casey M. Stuart, CPA, of Chattanooga, TSCPA Chair 1995-96; Gary Carden, owner of Carden Construction Company; Steve Kilenski, architect with Gresham Smith; Charles N. Dennard, CPA, of Nashville, TSCPA Chair 1994-95; Joe Thorne, CPA, of Cookeville, TSCPA Chair 1993-94; Brad Floyd, TSCPA President/CEO; Robert C. Brannon, CPA, of Nashville, TSCPA Chair 1975-76.

had begun on Sept. 25, and the completion of the building was scheduled to be April 1, 1996.

In 2014, David Morgan recalled TSCPA's decision to construct a permanent headquarters building in the Maryland Farms office park in Brentwood. He said, "There had been an ongoing discussion of a permanent home for TSCPA for a number of years vs. the continuation of renting office space. Frankly, for various reasons there were some members who were opposed to this idea. We pushed on, overcame the objections and got preliminary approval to get the project going. We bought the land at a time of depressed values and paid a very attractive price. Then, the building committee began its work and had the building designed. The committee was ready to propose the final go-ahead with the building for Council's approval, but at the last minute, a member of the building committee got cold feet, due to some unrest in the national economic situation. In spite of the staunch opposition of one member, others on the committee decided to push ahead and got the Council's approval to build the building. After it was complete, we placed a surcharge on our members' annual dues statement for a couple of years and also got the chapters to donate to a debt reduction effort. The end result was that the building was debt-free within a couple of years after it was built: a very successful project of which we should all be proud."

The interim Council meeting took place on Dec. 2 at the Opryland Hotel. Updates were provided by Stuart and Floyd on Society activities since the last meeting. David Morgan, Nashville Chapter president, and Tommy Greer, Appalachian Chapter president, presented TSCPA with chapter contributions totaling $115,000 ($100,000 and $15,000, respectively) to be used toward building construction. Ray Kamler presented an AICPA update, and Darrel Tongate presented a TSBA update.

May 3, 1996, was the date of the next Board meeting at the newly completed TSCPA headquarters, at 201 Powell Place in Brentwood. Floyd updated the Board on the recent move into the building, and the group toured the new facility. Brad Floyd recalls the events leading up to the completion of the headquarters building, saying, "In retrospect, the construction of a permanent headquarters building was one of the best business decisions made by the Society during the past 35 years. We've not only saved over $4 million in rent over the past 18 years, but the income generated from the meeting center has effectively paid for all occupancy costs during that time. There has also been a pride of ownership among the many members who visit it each year, and we're better able to brand TSCPA as a strong professional association when we host meetings that include elected officials and various governmental agencies. It proved to be a political challenge to gain the statewide support needed to complete the project, but thanks to the leadership of Billy Griesbeck, we were able to win TSCPA Council's support to secure prime real estate in 1993 at a very attractive price. And thanks to the leadership of Bob Brannon, David Morgan and Casey Stuart, we were able to complete construction of a first-class building in 1996 by using a creative loan package that was completely paid off within two years after construction. The building continues to serve the Society very well today, and it should continue to serve us well for decades to come."

> "In retrospect, the construction of a permanent headquarters building was one of the best business decisions made by the Society during the past 35 years. We've not only saved over $4 million in rent over the past 18 years, but the income generated from the meeting center has effectively paid for all occupancy costs during that time." - Brad Floyd

Later, the Board voted to contribute 50 cents per member to the Texas Society to defray the costs of their lawsuit against American

Express. Floyd also reported that the CPE program had recently completed 237 course days during the 1995 calendar year.

The regular Council meeting was held at the Opryland Hotel on June 17, 1996. The day before, the Society headquarters had hosted an open house and ribbon-cutting ceremony. Normal business was conducted with no new or significant issues brought forward.

The Board Workshop in 1996 was once again at Fairfield Glade. President Danny Pressley, of Knoxville, called the meeting to order on Aug. 16. A motion was passed to continue the $15 special dues assessment for the next Society fiscal year. Pressley asked the Board members to consider the issues of commissions and contingent fees in Tennessee. Phyllis Driver agreed to write an article for the *Journal* in order to provide members with more information on the topic. Pressley asked the Strategic Planning Committee to review the issue also. David Morgan made a motion that the Board of Directors request the president, executive director and appropriate committees develop a proposal to change the Tennessee accountancy law to allow the acceptance of commissions and contingent fees. The motion was duly seconded and passed unanimously.

TSCPA President 1996-97
J. Daniel Pressley

Morgan recalled, "The UAA had already been revised, and the AICPA had adopted the position that allowed for commission and contingent fees to be charged by CPAs. I held a strong position that CPAs needed to be open to other ways of being paid for their work rather than just hourly rates and proposed that we get the Tennessee state law changed to conform to the new UAA."

Jim Dunn, Chair of the Strategic Planning Committee, requested that the committee be renamed the Future Issues Committee and that the group would be charged with the responsibility of identifying future issues for Board consideration. He also recommended a change in the membership and structure of the committee. A motion to approve his recommendations was passed unanimously. The format of the Council meetings was discussed. The Board concluded that Council members should be educated on "hot topics or issues" during their meeting, and information material on these issues could be mailed to members before the meeting. Council format in the future could include panel discussions and roundtables, and perhaps CPE could be granted for attending Council.

> In 1996, the Board agreed unanimously to support a proposal that allowed for the acceptance of commissions and contingent fees.

Nov. 22 was the next meeting of the Board. The group discussed the pros and cons of maintaining the ban on commissions and contingent fees. Mark Layne and David Morgan agreed to present a report on the issue at the Dec. 7 Council meeting. A motion that the Board recommend to Council that the accountancy law be amended to mirror the AICPA rules on commissions and contingent fees was approved by a majority vote.

Layne recalled, "The concept of commissions and contingent fees had started to spread among the states. As discussions began on the Board, the feeling among board members was quite mixed. There certainly was not a consensus. So, we decided to take it to Council in a format whereby David Morgan would present the case against commissions and contingent fees, and I would present the case for commissions and contingent fees."

Political contributions from corporations to the Tennessee CPA PAC were also discussed. The Board agreed unanimously that any contributions received by way of corporate check would be determined to be intended as a contribution for the EMF scholarship program.

Council met on Dec. 7, 1996, at TSCPA headquarters for the first time. Wynne Baker presented an update on the AICPA Special Committee on Assurance Services, which planned to develop new independent professional services to be offered by CPAs in order to improve the quality of information, or its context, for decision-makers. Layne and Morgan presented a report on commissions and contingent fees. An open discussion by Council followed detailing the advantages and disadvantages of maintaining the current ban in Tennessee. A motion was passed by a majority vote for Council to support an amendment to the law that would eliminate the blanket prohibition against CPAs giving or receiving commissions or contingent fees. This current rule would be replaced by a limited prohibition against these fees involving audit/attestation clients. This proposed change would bring Tennessee law in conformity with the AICPA Code of Professional Conduct rules. Commissions and contingent fees would have to be disclosed to clients and could only be performed in dealing with non-audit/attestation clients.

According to Morgan, "With strong support from the Board and the Council, we were able to get that revision in the law made by the legislature. I seem to recall that Will Pugh helped a great deal with several key individual legislators."

Marietta Dodson-Pettibone was recognized by Council following the announcement of her retirement as the Society's CPE director on March 31, 1997. President Pressley presented her with a plaque commemorating her 24 years of service to TSCPA. Floyd reported that TSCPA had signed an agreement with Microsoft to establish a website for the Society in order to promote use of the Internet among CPAs in Tennessee. David Morgan recognized Floyd as the 1996-97 president of the CPA Society Executives Association. This was the association formed by all state society CEOs for the purpose of collaboration among all state CPA societies and representing the best interests of the CPA profession.

CHAPTER FOUR
1997-2001

Vision and Growth

As 1997 approached, the accountancy profession both nationwide and in Tennessee was dynamic, growing and looking to expand its service base. The scandals of the 1970s and 1980s had largely been forgotten, and both the AICPA and TSCPA were undertaking programs to propel the profession forward. TSCPA supplemented the AICPA national image improvement campaign by contributing $20,000 for ads designed to position CPAs as valuable business advisors. This was the first statewide advertising campaign TSCPA had done.

The National Association of State Boards of Accountancy (NASBA) and the AICPA Joint Committee on Regulation of the Profession had issued their report, which included a Uniform Accountancy Act (UAA). Brad Floyd was one of two state society executives appointed by the AICPA to serve on this joint committee charged with writing a new "model" state accountancy law. This act, if passed by state legislatures, would bring uniformity to the state regulation of the profession. One of the main tenets of the act would be to promote the portability of the CPA credential through the concept of "substantial equivalency." This proposal would allow CPAs to temporarily practice across state lines in person or via the Internet through reciprocity. The Tennessee Legislature had passed changes to the Tennessee Accountancy Act that allowed CPAs in Tennessee to accept commissions and contingent fees as long as there was no attest relationship with the client, and the client agreed to the fees in writing before the engagement began.

President Danny Pressley presided at the Board of Directors meeting on May 2, 1997, at TSCPA headquarters. The Board was updated on the new Tennessee Accountancy Act changes and the AICPA/NASBA Joint Committee proposal by Brad Floyd. They discussed the pros and cons of non-CPA ownership of CPA firms, but determined that further discussion was necessary in the future. They also reviewed plans for a Vision Project that would include a nationwide effort to create a vision for the future of the entire profession. They also passed a motion that changed the governance of the Nominating Committee slightly from the bylaw amendment that had been passed by Council in December 1994 that called for the chair of the Committee to be the past president in the final year of the three-year term rather than the first year.

> One of the main tenets of the Uniform Accountancy Act (UAA) was to promote the portability of the CPA credential through the concept of "substantial equivalency." This would allow CPAs to temporarily practice across state lines.

TSCPA announced the launching of its website, *www.tncpa.org*, in the June 1997 *Journal*. The primary goal of the site was to provide information to members on Society programs and activities. TSCPA developed the site to include information that would help members become information resources for their clients. The site included the CPE schedule, hotlinks, a careers and education section, marketing tips and "members only" content.

Council met on June 23, 1997, at the Grove Park Inn in Asheville, N.C. The Board amendment regarding the Nominating Committee was passed. Updates were given on TSCPA Board and TSBA activities. Sam Letsinger, Knoxville Chapter President, presented TSCPA with a $10,000 donation for the building fund. John Hunnicutt, AICPA Senior Vice President of Public Affairs, updated the group on the National Vision Project that would include a series of "future forums" in Tennessee to gather input from members.

The Vision Project aimed to pull the profession together to set a common course. Business (and the world) had changed dramatically with the development of technology; the Project was undertaken in order to keep CPAs relevant in this changing environment. Jeannie Patton, executive director of the Utah Society of CPAs, served as the national coordinator of the project. Nationwide, 165 Future Forums were held. In Tennessee, Future Forums were held in October and November in Memphis, Nashville and Knoxville. Society leaders from across the state gathered for daylong sessions to develop a vision for the profession in the year 2011. Participants at each site were asked to select from a list of values, services, competencies and issues and rank them in order of importance for CPAs. The entire group at each location then developed a consensus on each of these items. Delegates from 53 jurisdictions met in Phoenix on Jan. 12-13, 1998, at the National Future Forum to report the results. Danny Pressley served as the Tennessee representative at this forum. The resulting report contained the top five items for values, services, competencies and issues that CPAs, from a grassroots perspective, felt were the most important looking into the future. The Vision Project would become the focal point of activities of CPA professional organizations for years to come.

The AICPA Special Committee on Assurance Services issued its report in June 1997. This report had looked at the future of auditing and attestation services and decided these services needed to evolve into an "assurance function." Evidence from the time showed that audit revenues of the 60 largest CPA firms had steadily declined since 1989. The committee had identified six broad areas as potential "hot" services for CPAs. These were electronic commerce assurance, health care performance measurement, entity performance measurement, information systems quality, comprehensive risk assessment and elder care.

Fairfield Glade served as the location of the Aug. 22 Board meeting. The Board requested that Brad Floyd work with the TSBA to develop recommendations regarding implementation of the UAA in Tennessee. As a result, Floyd and Darrel Tongate, the TSBA executive director, held a series of meetings in the fall of 1997 to blend key elements of the Tennessee Accountancy Act with the new Uniform Accountancy Act. The Board also agreed that the TSCPA staff would plan all conventions beginning in the year 2000, with chapter support provided as requested.

Because of his contributions to the Joint UAA Committee and CPA Society Executives Association, Floyd was named by *Accounting Today* magazine to its list of Top 100 Most Influential People in Accounting in 1997. The magazine reported, "Floyd has a reputation among state society executives as one of the heavy lifters, able to handle the toughest jobs - like hammering out a new regulatory scheme and selling it to traditionalists."

The Board met on Nov. 21, 1997, at TSCPA headquarters. Wynne Baker, of Nashville, served as president for 1997-98. Floyd presented draft legislation that incorporated the major provisions of the UAA into the Tennessee Accountancy Act. The Board approved a proposal to request Council authorize the Board to pursue appropriate changes in the law. A task force comprised of President Baker, Ernie Baugh and Mark Layne was appointed to work with Society staff and the TSBA on the proposed legislation. The Board discussed the merits of the council policy that required cooperation with the Tennessee Federal Tax Institute (TFTI) to ensure a quality annual conference on federal taxation

TSCPA President 1997-98
Wynne E. Baker

to be held in the state. The group concluded it was not in the best interest of TSCPA to give preferential treatment to the Tax Institute over other outside groups. A motion was passed unanimously to recommend Council repeal this policy.

On Nov. 24, 1997, President Baker sent a letter to all members of the Board detailing concerns with the Tax Institute. He stated that TSCPA had been unable to develop a "partnership" with the group in order to jointly sponsor an annual tax conference, and therefore had started a TSCPA Federal Tax Conference. The letter continued that TSCPA had provided marketing support, mailing lists and other considerations in return for no direct benefits to TSCPA members. The TFTI Board of Trustees felt as if TSCPA should not have its own conference and that for 48 years the system had worked. Baker stated that TSCPA had changed significantly over that time, and the matter should not be ignored simply because "it's always been that way."

Council met on Dec. 6, 1997. Danny Pressley reported that three Future Forums had been held. Mark Layne reviewed the draft legislation to incorporate the UAA into the Tennessee Accountancy Act. He requested that Council authorize the Board of Directors to pursue appropriate changes in the Act, and Council voted the authorization. President Baker recommended that Council repeal the policy regarding the Tennessee Federal Tax Institute. A motion was then made to do so, and it passed unanimously. Additionally, at the request of the Knoxville Chapter, Al Kolak was elected an honorary member.

On April 1, 1998, Tennessee became the first state in the nation to enact the major provisions of the UAA when Gov. Don Sundquist signed the Tennessee Accountancy Act. The new law adopted the concept of "substantial equivalency" that allowed CPAs greater mobility to work across state lines. Non-CPA ownership of CPA firms (limited at 49 percent) was included in the law. The new act eliminated the "two tier" system of licensure and changed the experience requirement to earn a CPA license to one year. Restrictions were placed on the performance of attest services (audit, review and compilation) to registered CPA firms, and peer review was required for all firms offering these services. The legislation maintained the 80-hour biennial CPE requirement for all "active" CPAs, but those individuals wishing to avoid this rule would be classified as "inactive." The effective date of the legislation was Oct. 1, 1998. Governor Sundquist also declared April 16, 1998, as "CPA Appreciation Day."

On May 1, 1998, the Board of Directors met at TSCPA headquarters. David Morgan made a motion to pay off the balance of the term mortgage loan on the building, which was passed unanimously. Wynne Baker and Brad Floyd informed the group that the Accountancy Act had been passed. Danny Pressley updated the Board on the Vision Project.

The Council met at the Hyatt Regency in Knoxville on June 29, 1998, and the Board of Directors meeting was held on July 1. President

Tennessee Gov. Don Sundquist signs the Tennessee Accountancy Act of 1998, which conformed the Tennessee statute to the Uniform Accountancy Act endorsed by the AICPA. Witnessing the signing ceremony were State Rep. Randy Rinks; Dan Johnson, CPA, TSCPA Legislation Committee Chair; Wynne Baker, CPA, TSCPA President; Brad Floyd, TSCPA Executive Director; and State Sen. Ben Atchley.

Mark Layne, of Jackson, noted the upcoming Board Workshop. David Morgan reported that 14 TSCPA members had met with Sen. Fred Thompson and seven of Tennessee's representatives in Washington, D.C., and discussed issues important to CPAs nationally.

TSCPA President 1998-99
Mark M. Layne

The Board Workshop was held at Henry Horton State Park on Aug. 21, 1998. The Board discussed the dues structure of the chapters and compared TSCPA dues with other state CPA organizations. The Board acted to eliminate the state initiation fee for new members, and chapters were encouraged to do likewise. Board members provided updates from the committees for which they served as liaisons. Wynne Baker updated the Board on the Vision Project, and the Board adopted a resolution to support the Vision Statement, Core Purpose and Vision Elements of the Vision Project report (next page).

By late 1998, a growing concern was emerging both nationally and in Tennessee: the supply of CPA candidates. A total of 45 states had now adopted the 150-hour education requirement to sit for the CPA exam, and the number of candidates taking the exam was down significantly. In order to encourage students to major in accounting, the Board of Trustees of the EMF adopted new policies regarding scholarships in November 1998. First, at least one scholarship would be awarded to each university that has a student submitting a qualifying application. Second, they asked the Scholarship Committee to commit 20 percent of the available funds to students who are in the process of making a decision about their major, i.e., students who had completed introductory accounting courses at the sophomore level.

The interim Council meeting was held Dec. 5, 1998. Wynne Baker updated the members on the Vision Project. President Layne reported that Baker would represent TSCPA at the National

VISION PROJECT REPORT

Vision Statement: CPAs are the trusted professionals who enable people and organizations to shape their future. Combining insight with integrity, CPAs deliver value by:

    a. Communicating the total picture with clarity and objectivity.
    b. Translating complex information into critical knowledge.
    c. Anticipating and creating opportunities.
    d. Designing pathways that transform vision into reality.

Core Purpose: CPAs . . . making sense of a changing and complex world.

Vision Elements:

Core Values:
- **Continuing Education and Life-Long Learning**: CPAs highly value continuing education beyond certification and believe it is important to continually acquire new skills and knowledge.
- **Competence**: CPAs are able to perform high-quality work in a capable, efficient and appropriate manner.
- **Integrity**: CPAs conduct themselves with honesty and professional ethics.
- **Attuned to Broad Business Issues**: CPAs are in tune with the overall realities of the business environment.
- **Objectivity**: CPAs are able to deal with information free of distortion, personal bias or conflicts of interest.

Core Services:
- **Assurance and Information Integrity**: Provide a variety of services that improve and assure the quality of information, or its context, for business decision-making.
- **Technology Services**: Provide services that leverage technology to improve objectives and decision-making, including business application process, system integrity, knowledge management, system security and integration of new business processes and practices.
- **Management Consulting and Performance Management**: Provide advice and insight on the financial and non-financial performance of an organization's operation and strategic processes through broad business knowledge and judgment.
- **Financial Planning**: Provide a variety of services to organizations and individuals that interpret and add value by utilizing a wide range of financial information. These include everything from tax planning and financial statement analysis to structuring investment portfolios and complex financial transactions.
- **International Services**: Provide services to support and facilitate commerce in the global marketplace.

Core Competencies:
- **Communications and Leadership Skills**: Able to give and exchange information within meaningful context and with appropriate delivery and interpersonal skills. Able to influence, inspire and motivate others to achieve results.
- **Strategic and Critical Thinking Skills**: Able to link date, knowledge and insight together to provide quality advice for strategic decision-making.
- **Focus on Customer, Client and Market**: Able to anticipate and meet the changing needs of clients, employers, customers and markets better than competitors.
- **Interpretation of Converging Information**: Able to interpret and provide a broader context using financial and non-financial information.
- **Technologically Adept**: Able to utilize and leverage technology in ways that add value to clients, customers and employers.

Vision-to-Strategy Workshop. Council unanimously approved the elimination of the state initiation fee of $10, and also modified the policy requiring applicants for fellow or provisional membership to be sponsored by two fellow members. Committee and chapter reports were reviewed by the members.

Tennessee became the first state to implement the Quality Assurance Service (QAS) for CPE on Jan. 1, 1999. This rule mandated that licensees take self-study CPE from sponsors whose courses had been approved by the QAS. NASBA had established the QAS program in March 1998. Offerings from the AICPA or state societies were exempt from the rule.

On Jan. 11, 1999, the Board of Directors held a conference call to discuss legislation being proposed in Tennessee that would include (a) technical corrections to the Accountancy Act, (b) would clarify the confidential nature of information and (c) would separate the Board of Accountancy from the Division of Regulatory Boards. A quorum was not present for the call; therefore, any actions taken would be deemed recommendations. The participating members voted unanimously to support the proposed legislation that would clarify accountant-client privilege in Tennessee. They also voted to support the "decouple" aspect of the law, but only if it did not appear to jeopardize the passage of the privilege legislation.

> Tennessee became the first state to implement the Quality Assurance Service (QAS) for CPE on Jan. 1, 1999. This rule mandated that licensees take self-study CPE from sponsors whose courses had been approved by QAS.

President Layne appointed an ad hoc committee, the Special Committee on the Future Supply of CPA Candidates in Tennessee, to study the issue of the future supply of CPA candidates. The committee met on Jan. 22, 1999, at the TSCPA office and included Billy Griesbeck (chair), Claude Blankenship, Pam Church, Charles Frasier, Betty Price, Janice Smith, Casey Stuart and Dick Townsend. Brad Floyd and Darrel Tongate, the TSBA executive director, also attended the meeting. Tongate reviewed the 150-hour requirement and stated that under the current rule, all students must complete this requirement before applying to sit for the exam. The committee agreed that consideration should be given to allow candidates to sit for the exam during the semester in which they would complete the 150-hour requirement.

The Committee also noted that starting salaries for accounting graduates were generally lower than those of graduates from competing majors such as investment banking/finance, consulting and legal careers. Potential recommendations from the committee included: amending the Accountancy Act to permit students to sit for the exam during the semester in which they completed the 150-hour requirement, identifying better students in principles courses to encourage them to major in accounting, communicating the Vision Statement to high school career counselors, encouraging the chapters to work more closely with university accounting faculty, granting scholarships to high school students entering college as accounting majors, providing scholarships to college freshman and sophomores and providing a free or discounted membership to university faculty.

In the February/March issue of the *Tennessee CPA Journal*, it was announced that Connie Rhea had been promoted to assistant executive director after serving as the member services director for 16 years.

Nels T. "Ted" Moody, the former executive director of the Society, passed away on April 22, 1999. A donation to the EMF was made in remembrance of Colonel Moody. He had served as TSCPA's executive director from 1967 until his retirement in 1987.

The Public Relations Committee organized the Good Fortune Cookie Giveaway in the 1999 tax season. This program involved CPAs gathering at post offices and giving each person dropping off their tax returns on April 15 a fortune cookie containing the prediction "There is a CPA in your future - Tennessee Society of Certified Public Accountants." The Nashville Chapter had piloted the program the previous year and had received extensive media coverage.

The May 1999 *Tennessee CPA Journal* contained the highlights of *Public Accounting Report*'s annual survey of National Accounting Firms. The study showed that the largest CPA firms continued to chase big-margin consulting business and were relying less on accounting and auditing work. The Big Eight firms reported that 46 percent of revenue came from consulting, while auditing contributed 31 percent and tax 19 percent. Average partner revenue had increased 14.5 percent over the prior year.

Also in May 1999, the TSCPA Educational and Memorial Foundation's Board of Trustees approved a proposal to establish endowed scholarships in the names of contributors who pledge a minimum of $25,000. The first member to establish an endowed fund was Robert Knapp, of Memphis, and the Knapp Scholarship was established to provide support for the top accounting student from Shelby County.

> In May 1999, the EMF's Board of Trustees approved a proposal to establish endowed scholarships in the names of contributors who pledged a minimum of $25,000.

TSCPA media partnerships flourished during the 1999 tax season. Five television network affiliates partnered with TSCPA to provide tax hot lines. Over 2,600 calls were taken by 138 members who volunteered to work the hot lines. In addition, TSCPA and *The Tennessean* in Nashville co-sponsored an 11-week question-and-answer tax column.

The Board of Directors met on May 7, 1999, at Society headquarters. Dan Elrod updated the Board on legislative activity regarding accountant-client privilege and decoupling the TSBA. Elrod noted that the comptroller of the Treasury was concerned that the TSBA might be completely removed from regulatory authority. Wynne Baker updated the Board on the Vision Project and stated that he had spoken to almost all of the chapters on the issue. Floyd reported that a group of CPA societies were planning to develop a database for use in the development of interactive websites for the societies. The Board approved TSCPA to join the group at a cost of $5 per member.

The June 1999 Council meeting was held at the MeadowView Conference Center in Kingsport. Tony Jennings, treasurer, presented the financial statements and noted that the new TSCPA building was paid for and the Society was debt-free, with excess revenues over expenditures totaling approximately $170,000. President-elect Robbie McKinney, of Memphis, presented the AICPA Council report and advised TSCPA Council that the CPA exam would be computerized in the near future. Will Pugh reported on TSBA activities and stated that there were 11,000 CPAs in Tennessee, with approximately 7,700 actively practicing.

The AICPA Core Competency Framework for Entry into the Accounting Profession was announced on Aug. 16, 1999. This framework was designed to better prepare accounting students for entry into the profession. TSCPA member Paula Thomas, of Middle Tennessee State University, served on the group that developed the proposal. The plan called for a shift from a content-based curriculum to one that was "vision-based." It focused on developing the personal, functional and broad business perspectives of students and not just their technical accounting, auditing and tax skills. The TSCPA Accounting Education Committee sponsored a meeting in November at Belmont University to "educate the educators" about the proposal.

The Board of Directors retreat was held at Evins Mill in Smithville on Aug. 20, 1999. President Robbie McKinney presided. The Board discussed the current TSCPA dues structure with relation to other states. The Board reviewed the council policy covering the annual meeting and convention and proposed an amendment to Council that gave the Board of Directors responsibility for approving the schedule, program, promotion and all other arrangements for the convention. The amendment also gave the Board the right to establish convention fees and site selection. The previous policy had incorporated chapters in the convention planning and funding and had relied upon a rotation plan among the chapters for hosting the event.

The September 1999 *Tennessee CPA Journal* contained two articles that highlighted the technological events of the era. First, Y2K (Jan. 1, 2000) was creating anxiety among the population. Would

TSCPA President 1999-2000
Robbie A. McKinney

your information system work in the new millennium? Second, the AICPA, six information technology companies and the five largest professional services firms announced the development of an XML-based financial reporting language. This language (XFRML) would allow the financial community a standards-based method to prepare, publish, exchange and analyze financial reports in a freely licensed, uniform software.

In October 1999, the Tennessee State Board of Accountancy announced two major changes in the rules regarding CPE. Beginning in 1999, inactive licensees would no longer be required to obtain CPE. Active license holders were still required to earn 80 hours every two years. Of these, 40 were required to be in the technical categories of accounting/auditing, tax, computer science or management/advisory areas. A minimum of 20 hours must be completed each year. If an active licensee was engaged in the attest function, they would be required to obtain 20 hours in accounting/auditing. CPAs engaged in expert witness services must have 20 hours of CPE within the major subject area in which they were deemed to be witnesses. Teaching a course would earn a CPA three times the number of class hours, but was limited to 40 hours in each two-year period. Credit for reading the *Journal* was limited to 16 hours per period. Carryover CPE of up to 40 hours per period was allowed, and no limit was placed on self-study hours. A licensee would report the number of CPE hours when renewing, but detailed reports or documentation were not required to be filed unless the CPA was audited by the TSBA. Also effective for 1999, the 150-hour requirement was modified by stating that only 24 hours were required in both accounting courses and business courses. The previous rule required 30 hours in each.

The Board of Directors met on Nov. 19, 1999, at the Society headquarters. The only new business item was a request received from the New York Society of CPAs asking TSCPA to request the AICPA to attempt to legislatively resolve the problem of workload compression. The Board instructed TSCPA staff to draft a letter of support of the need for fiscal year reform.

The interim Council meeting was held on Nov. 20. Dan Elrod spoke about the 1999 special session of the Tennessee Legislature to review the state tax structure. Council voted to amend the Council policy regarding the annual meeting and convention. Committee reports and an EMF update were given.

The Tennessee General Assembly passed an amendment to the Accountancy Act in March 2000 that allowed CPA candidates who were within 120 days of completing the 150-hour requirement to sit for the CPA exam. This amendment addressed the issue of students who were taking the exam in other states that had not yet implemented the 150-hour requirement.

President McKinney called the Board of Directors meeting to order on April 28, 2000. David Morgan, TSCPA President-elect and an AICPA Council member, updated the group on two new initiatives. The AICPA planned to establish a vertical Internet portal in collaboration with state societies and outside investors. Also, the

AICPA had proposed a global credential that would be available to CPAs and fellow professionals in other countries.

This credential, the XYZ (placeholder name), would be created to reflect the changing nature of CPAs' work. According to the group proposing this credential, the CPA license was restricted by statutory regulations and was limited to the audit function. It no longer reflected all the work that members currently did and would do in the future according to the Vision Project. Also, "CPA" was not attracting enough students into the profession. XYZ was intended to be granted by eight of the world's leading professional organizations and would leverage the qualities of a CPA internationally.

> The General Assembly passed an amendment to the Accountancy Act in March 2000 that allowed CPA candidates who were within 120 days of completing the 150-hour requirement to sit for the CPA exam.

The Council was informed by President-elect Morgan that the annual Leadership Conference would be replaced with a Strategic Planning Workshop in the upcoming year. Approximately 30-40 Society leaders would be invited to participate in the workshop. Brad Floyd updated the group on the development of the CPAWEB.com Internet software and the formation of a Shared Service Corporation. The President's Cup criteria were discussed. In the past, the Cup went to the chapter with the largest percentage increase in membership for the prior year. President McKinney appointed a task force (Bernie Goldstein, Tony Jennings and Terri Jeter-McAvoy) to review the criteria and recommend alternatives to how the award was presented.

At the AICPA Council meeting on May 21-22, the Internet portal proposal (CPA2biz.com) was approved. The Shared Services

Corporation was formed in order to allow its partners to cooperate on efforts to provide comprehensive services and products to the CPA profession.

Robbie McKinney called her tenure as TSCPA president "the Dawning of a New Era," and her term saw numerous issues being discussed. The Vision Project, UAA, Cognitor, One Stop Shopping, Image Campaign and legislative issues dominated the conversation and led to strong debate over the issues. McKinney recalls, "A new way of thinking about the accounting profession and what CPAs do was emerging. My task was to expose the membership to these new concepts and enable members to make informed decisions about the future of our profession. I saw the future as a challenge to maintain our roles as the trusted business advisors and how we improve upon the image, as well as the continued need to brand the services that we do. I think our profession will be called upon to define over and over who a CPA is, and who those members that belong to this group will be. Future issues will be how to educate the next generation and what the CPA will look like in the future."

TSCPA President 2000-01
David K. Morgan

Council met at the Wyndham Palace Resort & Spa in Lake Beuna Vista, Fla., on June 19, 2000. Reports were given on recent Board and EMF activities, and Bob Elliott of the AICPA provided a professional issues update. Kevin Hickman was recognized as Committee Chairman of the Year for his work with the Public Relations Committee. The Board of Directors meeting on June 21 was led by President David Morgan, of Brentwood. The only new business conducted was the adoption of a position statement that opposed the enactment of a sales tax on services in Tennessee.

In August 2000, the *Tennessee CPA Journal* was first made available online to members. The TSCPA website had a new URL, *www.tscpa.com*, and other changes were made to the site to improve member services.

The Strategic Planning Workshop was held on July 19, 2000, and facilitated by Harrison Coerver. The current states of the profession and TSCPA were discussed, as well as the XYZ credential. Several recommendations came from the group that reflected the changing times. First, TSCPA must accelerate the use of technology to improve knowledge and information transfer among its members. Another priority that emerged was the need to re-evaluate the Society's governance structure. TSCPA policies should be adapted to reflect national and state issues such as multidisciplinary practice structures, the Internet portal, the XYZ credential and the Vision Project.

> In August 2000, the *Tennessee CPA Journal* was first made available online to members. The TSCPA website had a new URL, *www.tscpa.com*, and other changes were made to the site to improve member services.

The Board of Directors met on Aug. 25, 2000. David Morgan and Brad Floyd provided an update on professional issues, including the CPAWEB.com portal, the XYZ credential and a Securities and Exchange Commission proposal to revise the standards under which CPAs auditing public companies must operate. The Board proposed that TSCPA educate its members on the proposal and not take an official position.

The Board passed a motion to authorize TSCPA staff to void the contract with the Sandestin Hilton for the 2002 convention, look for an in-state location and restructure the convention. Attendance had been flat for years at the convention, and a nationwide trend among state societies had caused many to abandon the traditional annual conventions that were heavily composed of social events and family programming. The Board's desire was to discuss with Council the prospects of replacing TSCPA's traditional convention structure with an annual business meeting. President Morgan was to appoint a task force to work on the 2002 convention and re-evaluate the overall convention structure. Mike Uiberall requested the Board adopt a policy on committee term limits and continuity. Morgan assigned a task force of Uiberall (chair), Ernie Baugh and Tony Jennings to address this issue.

The Board may not have acted on the SEC proposal, but the AICPA was uniting the profession against it. In the September *Journal*, a request for action was made by the AICPA. The SEC's proposed rule change had been released in June 2000 and had contained new independence rules for CPAs auditing public companies. The rule proposed that CPA firms be prohibited from performing non-audit services to their audit clients. These services included accounting, financial systems design and implementation, and valuation, management, consulting, actuarial, human resources, financial planning, investment, legal and expert witness services. The proposal also restricted CPA firms from entering into joint ventures, partnerships and multidisciplinary practices. The AICPA stated that the proposal would disrupt effective relationships between audit firms and their clients when evidence existed that providing non-audit services to audit clients did not impair audit quality. The article asked CPAs to write their congressional representatives and contact the SEC stating their disapproval of the change.

The XYZ proposal was still being developed by the AICPA, but now it had a name: Cognitor. After extensive research and working with a branding company, the XYZ Global Task Force had proposed the name as meeting the requirements of the proposed credential. The proposed title would be placed in front of the professional's own name, e.g., Cognitor John Smith.

The next meeting of the Board of Directors was held on Nov. 17, 2000. Floyd and Morgan updated the Board on recent complaints that had been received from TSCPA members of a new TSBA rule that had limited self-study CPE to 50 percent of the total hours necessary. The Board took no action on this issue.

The Convention Task Force that President Morgan had created was comprised of Janice Smith (chair), Tony Jennings, Ernie Baugh, Ward Harder and Robbie McKinney. The task force reported to the Board and recommended that the annual membership meeting/convention and the Leadership Conference be combined into one annual event. The event would include an afternoon golf tournament to benefit the EMF and an evening reception, and be followed by a one-day leadership session/professional issues update. Awards would be presented at lunch, the annual member meeting would take place in the afternoon, and committees would meet. The Board approved the task force recommendations for the 2002 Nashville convention.

The interim Council meeting on Nov. 18, 2000, was highlighted by group breakout sessions. Members were asked to determine the three most important services provided by TSCPA. The results of the Strategic Planning Workshop had questioned the governance structure of TSCPA in terms of Council's role, selection of Board members and other organizational changes. Council members were asked if Council was an effective governing body and if certain governance responsibilities should be shifted to the Board of Directors. They were also asked if the selection process and structure of the Board should be changed. Finally, members were asked to reflect on other organizational issues such as chapters, committees and task forces.

In late 2000, the Tennessee State Board of Accountancy elected to defer the 50 percent limit on self-study CPE until Jan. 1, 2002, in order to study the issue in more depth.

The April 27, 2001, Board of Directors meeting started with President David Morgan discussing the XYZ Project and updating the group on the CPA2biz.com Internet portal. The Board voted unanimously to approve TSCPA participation in a Phase II agreement between the State Societies Network, Inc., and TSCPA for the purpose of granting the network certain non-exclusive rights to utilize the

TSCPA database and to establish a joint marketing agreement for the purpose of offering Info Bytes to TSCPA members.

The main agenda item at the meeting was the presentation of significant bylaw amendments that resulted from the governance discussions at the interim Council meeting the preceding November. These amendments would dramatically change the governance of TSCPA. In order to qualify for Life Membership, a member would have to have been a fellow member in good standing for 25 years, provide valuable service to TSCPA, and have reached the age of 65. Persons who had been members in good standing for 40 years would automatically qualify as a Life Member. Composition of Council would be revised to include the Board of Directors and not just the officers, as the bylaws had stated. The number of elected members of Council would be cut from 120 to 60 in order to improve the efficiency of the group. Past Society presidents would remain as lifetime members of Council. The Board of Directors would be expanded from 14 to 17 by adding three at-large members selected by the Nominating Committee. This was proposed to provide an opportunity to add members from diverse backgrounds. The Report Review Committee and the Bylaws Committee would be eliminated. Future bylaw amendments would be made by a special task force rather than the standing committee. The annual meeting of the Society would be required to meet within five months (not three) after the fiscal year end in order to hold the Leadership Conference (or convention) in July or August if needed. The required meetings of Council (currently two) would be reduced to one meeting annually. Finally, the requirement that student members had attained at least a junior standing would be eliminated in the hope that students would join earlier in their college careers. All these amendments were approved by the Board for consideration at the June 2001 Council meeting.

The Regular Council meeting was held on June 18, 2001, at the Adam's Mark Hotel in Memphis. AICPA Chairman-elect James Castellano presented a report on AICPA activities, including an update on the New Global Credential (the Cognitor name had been abandoned) and the CPA2biz.com portal. David Morgan presented the bylaw amendments to Council. A motion was passed by a majority vote to approve the slate of amendments for a vote by TSCPA membership.

Under new business, Council members discussed the Board's proposal to change the format of future annual meetings/conventions of the Society. A motion was passed by a majority vote of Council that instructed the Board of Directors to continue planning future conventions along the traditional formats of prior years.

Morgan considers the major re-write of the bylaws, including the reduction in size of Council, as his biggest achievement as president. During his term, the EMF had awarded the largest number of scholarships and total dollar amount in the history of the scholarship program (71 scholarships totaling $75,000). He enjoyed "getting to know other professionals from across the state," including, he says, "two individuals I met from Knoxville who ultimately became partners in our firm." He continued, "The profession is strong and will provide great opportunities for talented individuals in the future. CPAs are the trusted advisors to their clients and provide a wealth of knowledge that helps their clients solve problems and take advantage of opportunities in both their business and personal lives." He added that "the TSCPA does a great job of representing the profession in terms of enhancing our image and also plays a very important role in regulatory matters."

TSCPA President 2001-02
David A. "Tony" Jennings

The Board of Directors met on June 20, 2001, at the Adam's Mark Hotel. President Tony Jennings, of Kingsport, called the meeting to order. The Board discussed the annual meeting/convention issue and tentatively set the 2002 location at the Franklin Marriott Cool Springs. A motion was passed unanimously to mail the proposed bylaws amendment to members by Sept. 1, with the effective date of the changes (if approved by membership) being Jan. 1, 2002. The bylaws amendment ballot was mailed on Aug. 1 and remained open for 60 days.

The Board of Directors Workshop was held on Aug. 23-24 at Society headquarters. Board members provided chapter updates, and Jennifer Goggin (TSCPA communications manager) reviewed various services that the staff could offer to help chapters. The allocation of Council members given the new bylaws was discussed, and the Board requested the Nominating Committee meet via conference call if membership passed the bylaws change. Membership statistics as of Sept. 30 would be used to formulate the new Council allocation. Brad Floyd provided an update on the Shared Services agreement and the CPA2biz.com portal. He then updated the group on the XYZ credential. Floyd reported that the AICPA Council would vote to decide if a member ballot would be mailed to AICPA members to determine the fate of the program. The program would establish a separate, self-funded Global Institute to develop the infrastructure for a global business credential.

The week of Sept. 16-22, 2001, was designated "Accounting Week in Tennessee" by a resolution passed by the Tennessee Legislature on June 23 (opposite page). TSCPA supported this resolution and declared that the third week of September each year would be recognized as "Accounting Week." President Jennings used this opportunity to stress to the members that the new TSCPA Career Awareness campaign to encourage students to become CPAs was underway and that member involvement was crucial to its success. The AICPA had introduced a kit of curriculum materials, handouts, and a "Takin' Care of Business" video to be used by members when speaking to high school students.

Ninety percent of TSCPA members approved the proposed bylaws amendments, and they would become effective on Jan. 1, 2002. David L. Solomon, the winner of TSCPA's Outstanding CPA in

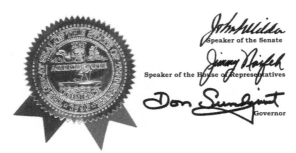

The Senate Resolution designating the third week of September as "Accounting Week in Tennessee," passed on June 23, 2001.

Business and Industry Award, was inducted into the AICPA Business and Industry Hall of Fame on Oct. 11, 2001.

In October, the AICPA Council voted 157-62 to support the Global Business Credential program. A membership ballot would be mailed on Oct. 29, and members would have 60 days to return it. Approval of two-thirds of the membership would be required for passage. The credential-granting organization would be named the International Institute of Strategic Business Professionals (IISBP). The entity's initials would be used to identify holders of the new credential; for example, John Smith, CPA, member IISBP, or John Smith, CPA-IISBP.

In October 2001, the accounting profession was vibrant, growing and looking forward to a bright future. The economy was being fueled by the dotcom boom, and CPA firms were offering a myriad of services to clients far beyond the traditional accounting, auditing and tax areas. The AICPA had approved the Vision Project, the Internet portal and a Global Business designation. Indeed, the times were quite good for the profession, until Oct. 16.

CHAPTER FIVE
2001-2004

Wreck and Recovery

On Oct. 16, 2001, Enron announced a $638 million loss for the third quarter. On Nov. 8, the company stated that it had overstated earnings by $586 million over the last four years and that it had $3 billion in obligations to various partnerships. The stock price plummeted from August 2000 ($90/share) to the end of October 2001 ($15/share). By Dec. 2, 2001, the value of a share was 26 cents. The firm's auditor, Arthur Andersen, would lose its federal trial on June 13, 2002, and shut down its operations on Aug. 31, 2002. In reaction to Enron and other financial scandals at WorldCom, Adelphia and Tyco, Congress subsequently passed the Sarbanes-Oxley Act (SOX) on July 30, 2002.

The Board of Directors met on Nov. 12, 2001. Mandy Young provided a legislative update to the members, and a motion was passed that the president form a committee that would deliver to the Board a proposed position on a state income tax. The Board approved the bylaws changes that had been approved by the membership vote. The Global Business Credential was discussed, and a motion was made that the Board take a position on the proposal and inform the membership of this position. The motion was seconded, but it did not pass for lack of a majority vote. Also approved was a $5,000 budget amendment to fund the Accounting Career Exposition, with Ward Harder serving as the chair of the event.

At the Nov. 17, 2001, Council meeting, no formal record of the scandal was recorded in the minutes, however, the "hallway talk" was all about Enron and its impact. The Council did review a video on the proposal to establish an Institute of International Business Strategic Professionals. They broke into groups to discuss the merits of the proposal. Ward Harder updated the Council on a joint project of the TSCPA Accounting Education and Career Awareness Committee and David Lipscomb University to hold an "Accounting Career Exploration Experience for High School Students" in July 2002, which went on to become Accounting Academy.

A major issue in the profession continued to be the recruitment of students. Through the efforts of numerous members, 70 presentations reaching more than 12,000 students in high school and college had been made in the previous year. The Society had also hosted the Tennessee Society of Accounting Educators in September in order to update university and college faculty about developments in the accounting profession.

In February 2002, the AICPA announced that membership had voted down the Global Business Credential. Of the approximately 134,000 ballots received, 62.7 percent voted against the proposal. Barry Melancon, AICPA President and CEO, stated that the membership had spoken and the Institute would not move forward with the program.

In the February/March 2002 issue of the *Journal*, President Jennings used his president's message to address the Enron scandal. He stated that the public trust must be restored and that TSCPA had been hard at work in doing so. The Society had coordinated live media interviews to clarify issues regarding professional standards. TSCPA was focused on upholding the reputation that CPAs had earned as the "most trusted business advisor."

The Board of Directors met on April 26, 2002, at the TSCPA office. Very little business was conducted, with the main topic of information being provided by Brad Floyd. He stated that the state CPA societies (represented by the State Society Network, Inc.) had been unable to reach a long-term contract with the Shared Services group and CPA2biz.com organizers, and that the temporary sponsorship between TSCPA and these groups would expire on May 30, 2002. The agreement was not renewed upon expiration.

> President Jennings addressed the Enron scandal, stating that the public trust must be restored and that TSCPA had been hard at work doing so. TSCPA was focused on upholding the reputation that CPAs had earned as the "most trusted business advisor."

On June 12, 2002, the Board of Directors held a conference call to discuss various issues. Ward Harder reported that 90 students had been invited to the Accounting Career Exposition, and a motion was approved to allocate an additional $20,000 contribution for the event.

Council met at the Franklin Marriott Cool Springs on June 20, 2002. Normal business was conducted, and J. Leigh Griffith was recognized as 2002 Chairman of the Year for his work on the Federal Tax Conference Committee. President-elect Ernie Baugh introduced AICPA President and CEO Barry Melancon, who provided an AICPA update on several issues, including the progress of legislation in Congress to regulate the profession. The AICPA had worked with Congress on a bill and had generally supported the Oxley (R-H.R.) version of the bill. Melancon felt confident that any bill passed by Congress regulating the profession would not be as detrimental to CPAs as previously feared. At the end of his presentation, while talking in the hallway, he received a call and immediately left the meeting; the news of WorldCom had broken. The resulting act was not as lenient toward CPAs as predicted by Melancon.

TSCPA President 2002-03
Ernest F. Baugh Jr.

The Board met the next day, with Ernie Baugh, of Chattanooga, assuming the role of president. For the first time, chapter presidents were invited to attend the meeting, and they updated the Board on the various activities their chapters had undertaken in the past year.

The first annual Accounting Academy was held July 14-17 at David Lipscomb University. A total of 52 high school students from across the state visited local accounting firms and area businesses, participated in interactive business case studies and heard presentations from Nashville business leaders. Students were very receptive to the program.

On July 25, 2002, Executive Director Brad Floyd was named the Association Executive of the Year by the Tennessee Society of Association Executives. This award was presented annually to a member who had demonstrated exemplary leadership and achievement on behalf of their association.

A TSCPA survey in mid-July was conducted, and 1,280 members responded. The members generally supported the reforms proposed in the Sarbanes-Oxley Act. In Tennessee, the primary concern was the "cascade effect." Various state legislatures across the United States had proposed laws that would incorporate many of the provisions of SOX to CPAs auditing private companies. Although SOX only applied to auditors of publicly held companies, this type of proposed legislation at the state level would be detrimental to local practitioners and the private companies they served. President Baugh wrote a series of articles in late 2002 in the *Journal* that assured members that TSCPA was monitoring this situation in Tennessee. No legislation to this effect was ever introduced in Tennessee.

The Board Workshop was held at Brasstown Valley Resort in Young Harris, Ga., on Aug. 5-6, 2002. A discussion of forming a new chapter in the Murfreesboro area resulted in a task force being assigned to study the issue. The task force members consisted of Rush Bricken (chair), Paula Thomas, Bob Whisenant and Barry Clouse. The group would draft a survey to be sent to interested parties to determine the desire of a new chapter. The Board discussed allowing non-CPAs to join the Society as associate members. Tony Jennings, Michael Uiberall and Barry Clouse were charged with studying the issues and reporting to the Board at the next meeting.

> The first annual Accounting Academy was held July 14-17, 2002, at David Lipscomb University. A total of 52 high school students from across the state visited local accounting firms and area businesses, participated in interactive business case studies and heard presentations from Nashville business leaders. Students were very receptive to the program.

The Board discussed the 150-hour rule and its impact on the supply of new candidates into the profession. The issue of finding and retaining qualified staff was still the number-one issue facing CPA firms, according to an AICPA national survey. In Tennessee, recruiting students to major in accounting and focusing on university accounting faculty were high priorities for the Society. Some talk of repealing the 150-hour rule had surfaced around the state a few years earlier, especially among practitioners having difficulty hiring a sufficient number of accounting graduates. Several individuals felt as if the 150-hour rule was scaring students away from the accounting major and that developing a 120/150 model would be a viable solution. This model would allow students to take the CPA exam after earning 120 college credits, but not earn their CPA license until completing 150 hours. After Enron and the resulting negative publicity to the profession, this talk had subsided because lessening the requirements to become a CPA after a national financial scandal would not be viewed favorably by the public.

The TSCPA Board had not taken a position on the 120/150 idea, yet they were still aware of the recruiting issue. Another concern was that, in addition to the decline in the number of candidates taking the CPA exam, the pass rates had dropped significantly. The Board wanted to take steps to improve the pass rate in Tennessee, and they passed a motion during the August meeting to recommend the TSBA increase the number of accounting hours required to sit for the exam from 24 to 30.

The Board was updated on the first Accounting Academy, and several suggestions were made by members. The group recommended the planning committee consider better promotion to high school educators, moving the camp among different universities/colleges and changing the name of the event.

Floyd reported to the Board that the TSCPA website had recently been honored with the "2001 Website Excellence Award" by the Tennessee Society of Association Executives.

On Sept. 4, 2002, Barry Melancon addressed the Yale Club about Enron and the Sarbanes-Oxley Act. It was his first speech to an outside audience since the act had been passed. He stated that the profession must reach back to its core roots and restore our most priceless asset: our reputation. The accounting culture had to be rejuvenated, and the AICPA was committed to assist in this reform. The scandal had been painful for the vast body of CPAs in public practice, and although a small majority had caused the problems, everyone in the profession had been affected. Melancon continued by stating there had been some inherent weaknesses in disciplinary and monitoring processes, but the Institute was committed to solve these problems and emerge from the scandal stronger than ever. The members of the AICPA were looking forward to implementing the fundamental reforms of SOX and looking forward to continuing the role of CPAs as trusted business advisors and protectors of the public interest.

The task force charged with evaluating the possibility of forming a new TSCPA chapter headquartered in Murfreesboro, which would be comprised of the Upper Cumberland Chapter, the Elk Valley Chapter and a portion of the Nashville Chapter, reported their findings at the November Board meeting. The group, along with Brad Floyd and Connie Rhea, met in Murfreesboro to discuss the results of a survey they had conducted about the issue. The task force concluded that there was insufficient "critical mass" of members in the proposed geographic area that would be necessary to sustain sufficient leadership and participation levels. The group agreed to continue to gather member feedback on the possibility of the Elk Valley Chapter and/or the Upper Cumberland Chapter being absorbed into the Nashville Chapter with enhanced chapter services being delivered to these outlying areas.

The Board of Directors met on Nov. 22, 2002, at Society headquarters. President Baugh appointed Bob Whisenant, David Haddock, Greg Gilbert and John Griesbeck to serve on a task force to examine the TSCPA dues structure. Rush Bricken reported on the Elk Valley Chapter realignment, and the Board concluded there was not enough information at the time to make a decision. The Realignment Task Force was instructed to continue to study the issue and report at the April 2003 meeting. Members were informed that the TSBA had decided not to change education requirements to sit for the CPA exam. Harold Monk, AICPA Board member, updated the group on various Institute initiatives, including image enhancement, student recruitment, SOX and CPA2biz.com.

The interim Council meeting took place on Nov. 23, 2002. Monk reviewed AICPA activities for the group, and members broke into smaller groups to discuss the image enhancement program in order to provide feedback to Monk. Chapter representatives updated the Council on their activities. Mike Costello, Chattanooga Chapter President, presented a $4,000 contribution to the Educational and Memorial Foundation for the 40 chapter members who had pledged as Life Associates. He also announced that the chapter was contributing an additional $25,000 to establish a Chattanooga Chapter endowed scholarship. Brad Floyd was recognized by the group for his 25 years of service to the Society.

In January 2003, the AICPA Board of Examiners announced that the CPA exam would become computerized starting in May 2004. They also changed the format of the exam to four sections (Auditing/Attestation, Regulation, Financial Accounting & Reporting and Business Environment and Concepts) and reorganized some of the content. The exam would be offered in four two-month testing windows throughout the year, and candidates would be allowed to take the exam one part at a time and in any order they wanted. Final acceptance of this proposal would depend on the individual state boards of accountancy.

The Tennessee State Board of Accountancy had made several rule changes at its November 2002 meeting that were reported in the February/March issue of the *Tennessee CPA Journal*. The new rules required CPAs performing professional services, including those who are not members of the AICPA, to conform to the independence standards of the TSBA, the AICPA, the SEC, the General Accounting Office and other regulatory or professional bodies. The TSBA also passed a rule that a licensee must retain work papers for a five-year period commencing at the end of the fiscal period in which the engagement was conducted.

In April 2003, the AICPA announced it was foregoing its national image enhancement program and instead was going to focus on individual states to implement the campaign. A series of three ads, each featuring the tagline "America Counts on CPAs," were provided to the state societies in order to embark upon a more grassroots enhancement effort.

The Board of Directors met on April 25, 2003, with President Baugh presiding. Board members provided updates on the committee for which they served as liaisons. Michael Uiberall, on behalf of the TSCPA Federal Tax Committee, made a motion to make Etoile Bellar an honorary member of TSCPA due to her involvement and support of the profession. Bellar was an IRS employee who provided help and assistance to practitioners and the TSCPA Federal Taxation Committee. The motion was passed by the Board. The Board also passed a motion to request the Accounting Education Committee to consider rotating the Accounting Academy around the state every four years.

> The EMF experienced significant growth in the years after taking over the CPE function from the Society. Along with the success of the Life Associate Program, this increased the amount of scholarships awarded each year substantially.

The group discussed the existence of the Elk Valley Chapter, and chapter representative Rush Bricken reported the chapter membership would like to continue one more year to determine the viability of the chapter. The Board discussed the need to have a fall meeting of Council and determined that the July Council meeting agenda would include a discussion regarding the need for the fall meeting. The Public Relations Committee was asked to review TSCPA criteria for the Presidents' Cup and offer recommendations to the Board on whether or not to continue the award. Brad Floyd stated that some implementation dates for the Shared Services group were being delayed.

The Educational and Memorial Foundation had experienced significant growth since taking over the CPE function from the Society. Gross receipts from the program had surpassed $1 million for the first time in 1996. By 2003, the gross receipts from offering CPE programs was $1,875,575. Given this growth and the success of the Life Associate Program, the amount of scholarships awarded each year had increased substantially.

TSCPA Council met on July 17, 2003, at the Chattanooga Marriott. Normal business was conducted, including approval of the financial statements and the Nominating Committee report. President Baugh updated the group on Board activities since the last Council meeting, as well as the activity of the EMF Board of Trustees. During open forum, Council members discussed the need for a meeting of Council at both the annual meeting/convention and during the fall. Based on the discussion, it was decided to continue the two meetings in the future. A brief Board of Directors meeting was held the next day, with Greg Gilbert, of Knoxville, assuming the role of president. Chapter representatives updated the Board on the activities of each of the chapters.

TSCPA President 2003-04
G. Gregory Gilbert

The Board Workshop was held Aug. 20-22 at Fairfield Glade. Following a discussion on the current dues structure, a decision was made not to make any changes, but the task force was instructed to continue to study the issue and to compare TSCPA's structure with other state societies. The Board was updated on the 2004 Accounting Academy and encouraged the organizing committee to develop a process to track camp participants to see if they had chosen accounting as a career. The Board recommended that the camp be held at Lipscomb for no more than five years (including the past two years) and that other schools in the Nashville area be considered for future camps. Mark Steadman, Accounting Education Committee Chair, updated the group on two new proposals the Committee planned to undertake in the coming year: a high school educators' forum and a high school liaison program. The Board approved both programs.

Bill Reeb facilitated the strategic planning session during the workshop. The primary focus of this session was to develop a new mission statement and vision for TSCPA going forward. After several hours of small group discussion and analysis, a task force was created to complete the project. Mike Cain (chair), Betty Price, John

U.S. Sen. Lamar Alexander meets with TSCPA representatives during a congressional visit to Washington in 2003. From left are: John Griesbeck, CPA, of Memphis; Paula Thomas, CPA, of Murfreesboro; Senator Alexander; Will Pugh, CPA, of Knoxville; and Bob Whisenant, CPA, of Nashville.

Griesbeck, Sam Letsinger and David Haddock served as members of the task force.

Dec. 5, 2003, was the date of the next Board meeting. A motion to recognize Darrel Tongate for his service to the State Board of Accountancy was passed. Mike Cain presented the report of the Mission Statement Task Force, which recommended the adoption of a new mission statement. The proposed mission statement was: "The mission of the Tennessee Society of Certified Public Accountants is to enhance the success of our members through service, support and advocacy." The Board unanimously passed a motion to adopt this statement and proposed to Council to adopt it also.

Council met on Dec. 6 at TSCPA headquarters. President Gilbert summarized the activities of the Board since the last Council meeting. Mike Cain presented the Board-recommended mission statement to Council members, which, given no objections, would become effective on April 23, 2004. Updates were presented on legislation, as well as state board and AICPA activities. David Costello, NASBA president, addressed the members on several initiatives they were undertaking. Council members then broke into groups to discuss professional and regulatory issues, with the primary focus being on an AICPA proposal to develop Private Company Financial Reporting standards.

On Jan. 29, 2004, TSCPA celebrated its 100th anniversary. The Society had grown from its original membership of seven to 7,704 (as of Nov. 1, 2003). There was neither permanent office space nor staff in the beginning. Original dues had been $6 per year. As of March 31, 2004, TSCPA had annual budgeted revenue of $1,035,900. The profession had changed, and the Society had promoted that change for a century. Through TSCPA advocacy and support, CPAs in Tennessee were successful and the future was bright.

> The Mission Statement Task Force recommended the adoption of a new mission statement, "To enhance the success of our members through service, support and advocacy." The Board unanimously passed a motion to adopt this statement.

Reflecting on his term as president, Gilbert said, "From a personal standpoint, I most cherish the tremendous network of friends and lifelong relationships that I developed during my travels around the country on behalf of the Society. However, from a business standpoint, I most value the work done by TSCPA to protect the CPA license in Tennessee. TSCPA stands alone in representing CPAs in the state legislature and on regulatory matters, uniting the profession as a whole to create a coordinated voice. Our track record of legislative success over the years has clearly placed Tennessee as a leader in adopting uniform standards and protecting the CPA brand."

President Gilbert presided at the Board of Directors meeting on April 23, 2004. Gilbert reminded the Board that the new mission statement was automatically adopted at this meeting. Dan Elrod provided a legislative update. No new business was discussed.

In May 2004, the AICPA launched the 360 Degrees of Financial Literacy program. The program was designed to assist American households in adequately planning for their current and future financial needs.

Council met on June 14, 2004, at the Wild Dunes Resort in Isle of Palms, S.C. President Gilbert updated the group on Board and EMF activities. The Memphis Chapter presented a check for $5,000 to the Educational and Memorial Foundation.

TSCPA President 2004-05
John M. Griesbeck

John Griesbeck, of Memphis, became TSCPA president for 2004-05. The Board of Directors, under his leadership, met on June 16, 2004. The Board discussed a joint convention with a surrounding state, but no action was taken. The Board also approved a concept to establish a comprehensive marketing partnership with First Tennessee Bank. In 2014, Griesbeck said, "As I recall my experience as President, it was a great year that I will always look back on, not so much for what was accomplished, but just for having the opportunity to serve a great Society such as ours. My best memories are of all the members I met at Chapter meetings across the state and other events representing the Society. This would include the AICPA Council meetings, where it quickly became apparent how respected our state is around the country. Also, you learn quickly how talented and dedicated our Society staff are when you work with them closely over the course of a year. Brad's leadership and Connie and all of our staff are second to none. Another remembrance is just how quickly the year passed. By the time I wrote something for the *Journal* or did a presentation, another month had flown by and the year that began at Wild Dunes closed quickly at the convention in Johnson City. Lastly, I would say that those years were some of the most enjoyable of my career because I felt we were always working to improve the Society for its members and advance the profession in Tennessee. I made many friends during that time and have always said that if my car broke down between Memphis and Bristol, I could easily find a TSCPA member to help me out along the way."

The TSCPA Board of Directors Workshop was held on Aug. 18, 2004, at the Chattanoogan. The Board discussed several proposals to address the continuing problem of low student enrollment in accounting programs across the state. The staff was instructed to submit a proposal to develop a Young CPA Conference to be held in 2005. The Board discussed potential initiatives to engage young/new CPAs in the Society. These included establishing a Young CPA Task Force, adding a new CPA to each committee and to the Board, starting an advisory group with a representative from each chapter, a mentoring program and a Young CPA electronic newsletter.

The AICPA "CPA Ambassador Program," which was designed to train CPAs as spokespeople to promote the profession in their respective communities, was discussed. Griesbeck, Brad Floyd and Connie Rhea agreed to identify a pool of 10 members to participate in the program. A motion was passed that requested the Elk Valley Chapter prepare a report on the future structure of the chapter for presentation at the next Board meeting. The Board also approved the placement of a plaque in TSCPA headquarters acknowledging the service of past presidents of the Society.

The Board of Directors met on Nov. 19, 2004, at headquarters. They were updated on the activities of the Accounting Education & Career Awareness Committee, including the Accounting Academy, the High School Liaison Program and the High School Educators Symposium. President Griesbeck provided an AICPA update. The CPA Ambassador training program had been scheduled for Feb. 8, 2005. Bob Whisenant reported that a New CPA Conference would be held in conjunction with the Leadership Conference on Aug. 5, 2005.

The Council meeting on Nov. 20 was filled with updates; the activities of the AICPA, the State Board, the legislature, the Board of Directors, the EMF Board of Trustees, the Political Action Committee, the chapters and various committees were presented. No new action was taken. The Society and the profession were moving into a less hostile, post-Enron environment. After surviving Congressional action, the CPA profession was once again moving forward, and the business of TSCPA was getting back to normal.

CHAPTER SIX
2005-2009

Expanding Possibilities

As 2005 began, three issues were still on the front burner for TSCPA: the supply of CPA candidates, restoring the public confidence in CPAs and financial literacy. Several activities were undertaken by the Society to address these issues. On Feb. 11, 2005, TSCPA held a one-day High School Educators' Symposium. Twenty-five teachers from throughout Tennessee attended the event, which was designed to inform them of the opportunities the CPA profession offered. Each educator was given materials introducing them and their students to the accounting profession. TSCPA had also developed a High School Liaison Program intended to provide every high school in Tennessee with a member to serve as the direct contact for the school. In the first year of the program, members had volunteered, and over 40 percent of the high schools in Tennessee had a liaison.

On Feb. 8, 2005, nine members attended the CPA Ambassador training program at TSCPA headquarters: Greg Gilbert, John Griesbeck, Kevin Hickman, Tony Jennings, Terri Jeter-McAvoy, Janice Smith, Kathy Watts, Bob Whisenant and Louis Wright. The program was designed to provide hands-on, top-quality spokesperson training. The AICPA developed the program as a method to inform the public of the enduring value of the CPA and to rebuild the confidence of the public in CPAs.

The 360 Degrees of Financial Literacy program was in full swing, and a variety of materials were made available to members. An online resource center, *www.aicpa.org/financialliteracy*, was established by the AICPA, with toolkits for CPAs to use in assisting their clients. Mobilization kits containing PowerPoint presentations and other materials were available to CPAs to use in group settings. The consumer website, *www.360financialliteracy.org*, was developed for individuals wanting more information.

The Board meeting on April 29, 2005, provided the group the opportunity to review the strategic plan that had been developed the previous August. The Board also voted to increase the check-off on the annual dues statement for the PAC and EMF from $25 to $30 per year.

Council met on June 23, 2005, at the Carnegie Hotel in Johnson City. Leslie Murphy, AICPA Chair, provided a professional issues update. Normal Council business was conducted, but no new business was discussed. The Board meeting on June 25 was brief, with no new business introduced.

The New CPA Conference was held on Aug. 5, 2005, at the Nashville Convention Center in conjunction with the TSCPA Leadership Conference.

TSCPA President 2005-06
Robert V. Whisenant

The Board of Directors Workshop was held at Barnsley Gardens in Adairsville, Ga., on Aug. 24-26, 2005. The Board discussed public statements of TSCPA, and President Bob Whisenant, of Nashville, appointed Jim Myers (chair), Andy Bonner and Barry Clouse as a task force to study the issue. Paula Thomas presented an AICPA update to the Board that included a discussion of Private Company Financial Reporting, image enhancement, career initiatives and peer review transparency. The Board voted unanimously to endorse the recommendations of the AICPA Private Company Financial Reporting Task Force and encourage changes to GAAP for privately held entities.

The Board discussed the shortage of Ph.D. candidates, as well as scholarships and aging accounting educators. President Whisenant appointed a task force consisting of Louis Wright (chair), Janice Smith, David Haddock and Andy Bonner to study the issue and report at the November Board meeting. A state board update was provided by Linda Biek, TSBA Executive Director, and Doug Warren, TSBA Chair. A state board proposal to amend the Accountancy Act to allow candidates to sit for the CPE exam after completing a bachelor's degree (the 120/150 proposal) was deferred by the TSCPA Board until the November meeting. At this time, 31 CPA jurisdictions had implemented the 150-hour rule, 17 had adopted a 120/150 model, and six operated without the 150-hour rule.

Just a few years earlier, the profession had been faced with a decline in the number of accounting graduates, and several TSCPA programs had been implemented to address this issue. The problem in 2005 was different: accounting enrollments at universities and colleges in Tennessee were increasing, but fewer accounting graduates were taking the CPA exam. While no one truly understands the mind of college students, many felt as if the enrollment increase was due in part to the publicity (however negative) the profession had gotten during the Enron scandal. However, the number of individuals sitting for the exam was troubling, and many felt that the 150-hour requirement was a principal reason. Nationwide, there had been a 37 percent decline in candidates sitting for the exam between 2003 and 2004. In Tennessee, the state board reported a 65 percent decline during this same period.

The Board was updated on the upcoming Financial Literacy Week in Tennessee. A motion was passed to amend the budget to include $15,000 to produce a calendar to be distributed during the week. Kevin Hickman (chair), Sam Letsinger and Bob Palmer were appointed by President Whisenant to review and approve the calendar.

The possibility of adding an "affiliate membership" for non-CPAs who maintain business relationships with CPAs was discussed. A task force (John Griesbeck, Mike Cain and Lynn Battles) was appointed to review the issue and recommend a proposal at the November meeting. The Board once again requested the Elk Valley Chapter to prepare a report on its future structure and present the report at the November meeting, and it was passed. The Board unanimously voted to increase the voluntary dues check-offs for EMF and PAC to $35. Also approved was a motion that David Lipscomb University (soon to be just Lipscomb University) and Belmont University submit requests for proposals to the Society to serve as host of the high school Accounting Academy beginning in 2007.

The week of Oct. 16-22, 2005, was proclaimed "Financial Fitness Week" in Tennessee by Gov. Phil Bredesen. In six chapters across the state, TSCPA volunteers set up booths in malls, YMCAs and recreation centers to distribute the Financial Fitness calendars and other materials. TSCPA members also answered any questions from individuals visiting the booths.

In November 2005, the Tennessee State Board of Accountancy proposed new rules that would require CPAs to earn at least four hours of CPE every two years in ethics training. The requirement became effective in January 2006, and TSCPA developed a course that met the requirements of the rule, which was offered to members during 2006.

The Board of Directors met on Nov. 18, 2005, at Society headquarters. Jim Myers, Chair of the Public Statement Task Force, reported a proposed policy to the group, but no action was taken. Kevin Hickman, Chair of the Financial Literacy Task Force, reported that the third week of October had once again been designated as "Financial Literacy Week" in Tennessee, and TSCPA would distribute customized calendars to commemorate this event.

The task force chaired by John Griesbeck studying affiliate memberships reported to the Board. They recommended that if such a membership category was approved, it should be restrictive and follow specific guidelines. These guidelines included eligibility requirements, a policy that the affiliate member could not vote on Society matters nor hold an officer position or serve as a committee or task force chair. The Board took no action on this proposal.

> In November 2005, the Tennessee State Board of Accountancy proposed new rules that would require CPAs to earn at least four hours of CPE every two years in ethics training. The requirement became effective in January 2006, and TSCPA developed a course that met the requirements of the rule.

The interim Council meeting was held on Nov. 19, 2005, at TSCPA headquarters. President Whisenant updated the group on the Board of Directors' activities, Dan Elrod provided a legislative update, Paula Thomas gave an update on AICPA actions, and Linda Biek reported on recent activities of the Tennessee State Board. Wanda Jones, TSCPA's finance director, was recognized for her 25 years of service to the Society. Council members broke into small groups to discuss the decrease in the number of candidates sitting for the CPA exam.

Several suggestions were developed by the small groups that were summarized in the December 2005 *Journal*. These included the overall conclusion that accounting educators, CPA firms and other employers of CPAs must do a better job of communicating the importance of the exam. CPA firms should establish a system of monitoring candidates' preparation, scheduling and completion of the exam. Firm policies should encourage staff to complete the exam within 12-18 months, require staff to take one section of the exam in each testing window, reimburse staff for testing expenses, give staff paid time off to take the exam and reward completion of the exam with a bonus.

The group at the November Council meeting also discussed the need to create a task force to study the 120/150 proposal. President Whisenant agreed to form a group to study the issue and report to Council.

An issue developing in Tennessee in late 2005 was peer review program transparency. The program had been started 30 years earlier as a remedial, not disciplinary system. State societies, including TSCPA, administered the program. Regardless, in May 2004, the AICPA Council had passed a resolution that the peer review results should be transparent and the results be made available to the public and the state boards. NASBA had asked that the state boards be allowed unfettered access to the review results, and several state society members felt as if this proposal would be detrimental to the success of the program. In February 2005, the AICPA had appointed a task force to propose changes to the program. In Tennessee, the state board rules in 2005 provided for strict confidentiality of the peer review results, and that neither third parties nor the state board had access to the reports. The accountancy law still required that all CPA firms be enrolled in an approved practice monitoring program.

Another issue gaining attention in early 2005 was the outsourcing of work by public accounting firms, specifically for tax returns. The AICPA had updated its Code of Professional Conduct to provide guidance for practitioners that outsourced work. The new rules allowed this practice as long as the CPA informed the client that their tax return may be prepared by someone outside the CPA firm. However, the CPA did not have to disclose the fact that the return may be prepared by someone outside the United States (primarily in India). Proponents of the system felt that outsourcing helped alleviate overworked employees, lowered costs and had the necessary security to be trusted. Opponents of the system felt as if it cheapened the image of tax preparation and the public's view of the profession. The results of a survey of Tennessee CPAs were published in the February/March issue of the *Tennessee CPA Journal*. The survey showed that 95 percent of Tennessee CPAs did not outsource work, and that 90 percent felt the practice was not good for the profession.

The second CPA Ambassador Program was held at TSCPA headquarters on March 2, 2006. Participants were Wynne Baker, Michael Cain, David Curbo, David Haddock, Anita Hamilton, Jim Lloyd, Robbie McKinney, Jim Myers and Mark Steadman.

A conference call of the Board of Directors was held on March 6, 2006, to discuss a proposal from the Tennessee Federal Tax Institute's board of trustees. The TFTI's board had requested that the TSCPA Federal Tax Conference be combined with the TFTI's annual conference in the future. The TSCPA Board unanimously approved that President Whisenant and Brad Floyd move forward with the negotiations to merge the two conferences. The two conferences were subsequently merged under the direction of TSCPA, and the new conference was called the Tennessee Federal Tax Conference.

The next Board of Directors meeting was on April 28, 2006. Greg Gilbert, Chair of the 120/150 Task Force, presented a report on the proposal to allow CPA exam candidates to take the exam after completing a bachelor's degree, with certification coming after completion of 150 hours. Gilbert reported that the task force recommended continued monitoring of the rule, but that it had no recommendation to change the rule at this time. The Board accepted this recommendation and asked the task force to request input from accounting academic programs in Tennessee as they continued to gather information.

Brad Floyd updated the group on the proposed merger of the TSCPA Federal Tax Conference with the Tennessee Federal Tax Institute and reported that one conference would be held annually, beginning in December 2007. Louis Wright, Chair of the Scholarship Task Force, presented the results of the task force's work and reported that they recommended no changes to the scholarship program at this time. The new lottery scholarships had begun in Tennessee, and questions had been raised about the TSCPA scholarship awards in light of the lottery funds. The task force had surveyed accounting professors across the state in late 2005, and the results of that study had led the group to this conclusion.

The AICPA created the Special Committee on Mobility to investigate issues that prevented CPAs from practicing in states other than the one in which they were licensed. The "substantial equivalency" concept was not operating as envisioned, because 34 states had enacted their own version of the rule, thus diluting this provision of the Uniform Accountancy Act and making it difficult for CPAs to practice across state lines without obtaining another state license. The special committee was charged with determining methods to eliminate artificial barriers to interstate practice that, in the current environment, did nothing to protect the public interest.

The Peabody Hotel in Memphis was the location for the June 26, 2006, Council meeting. Council members were provided with updates on Board, EMF, chapter and committee activities. The Chattanooga and Memphis chapters each presented checks for $5,000 to the EMF. The Board met briefly on June 28 under the direction of the new president, Louis Wright, of Chattanooga, as a planning session for the upcoming year. They did discuss peer review transparency, but agreed to continue the discussion in depth at the August meeting.

TSCPA President 2006-07
Louis S. Wright

The August 2006 Board of Directors Workshop was held at Barnsley Gardens in Adairsville, Ga. Paula Thomas provided an AICPA update to the Board. Linda Biek and Doug Warren, representing the TSBA, updated members on the activities of the State Board. Greg Gilbert, Chair of the 120/150 Task Force, presented a recommendation that the Tennessee Accountancy Act be amended to allow CPA candidates to sit for the exam within 200 days of completing the 150-hour requirement. This proposal was a compromise position that maintained the 150 hours but allowed individuals an earlier window in which to sit for the exam. The Board passed this recommendation with a majority vote.

The Board was informed that a firm directory providing key information about CPA firms in Tennessee was being created. After reviewing the RFPs, a motion was made to choose Lipscomb University as the site for the 2007 high school Accounting Academy. The motion was seconded but failed. A motion was then made to move the program to Belmont University for one year and request another RFP for 2008. This motion was passed by majority vote. Jamie Compton, TSCPA communications manager, updated the Board on the new AICPA partnership with the Ad Council to produce, distribute and promote a public service campaign. This campaign would focus on financial literacy and use the tagline "Feed the Pig." The campaign launch date was set for Oct. 24, 2006.

At the meeting of the Board of Trustees of the Educational and Memorial Foundation held at the workshop, Brad Floyd announced a new scholarship in memory of Maxie Patton, who had recently passed away and had left a legacy of service to the accounting profession and TSCPA. He had served as TSCPA president, as a member of AICPA Council and for five terms as a member of the Tennessee State Board of Accountancy, including five years as chair. The scholarship would be awarded annually to the top accounting student at Tennessee Tech University.

"Feed the Pig" was launched on Oct. 24 and featured an adult-sized pig, Benjamin Banks, as the promotional mascot. The program was aimed at 25- to 34-year-old individuals in the attempt to educate the group about the importance of saving money. The "Feed the Pig" initiative was an outgrowth of the 360 Degrees of Financial Literacy Program and featured TV, radio, print, digital and outdoor mediums. TSCPA promoted the program within the state.

Tennessee State Board of Accountancy rule changes became effective on Oct. 26, 2006. The licensing fee for CPAs was raised from $80 to $120 every two years. The four-hour ethics CPE requirement was being phased in and would become fully operational in 2008. Licensees were allowed to carry forward 24 hours of CPE into the next reporting cycle.

> A new scholarship was established in memory of Maxie Patton, who left a legacy of service to the accounting profession and TSCPA. The scholarship would be awarded annually to the top accounting student at Tennessee Tech University.

On Dec. 1, 2006, the Board of Directors met at Society headquarters. The main item of business was the 120/150 rule. The 120/150 task force activities were provided, and a motion was made to keep the current law in place regarding sitting for the CPA exam. For lack of a majority vote, the motion did not pass. On a separate motion, the Board recommended that the Accountancy Act be amended to allow CPA candidates to sit for the exam within 200 days of completing the 150-hour requirement. The motion passed unanimously and was presented to Council the next day.

The interim Council meeting was held on Dec. 2, 2006, at TSCPA headquarters, with President Louis Wright presiding. Normal updates on AICPA, State Board, Board of Directors and EMF activities were provided. Council members then broke into groups to discuss the 120/150 task force recommendation that candidates be allowed to sit for the CPA exam 200 days before completing 150 hours. After the group discussion, Council reconvened and voted to approve the proposal to amend the Accountancy Act.

The once anemic Educational and Memorial Foundation was now flourishing. At the end of 2006, the endowment fund balance surpassed $1 million for the first time. In other news, in January

2007, TSCPA announced that members would be able to pay their dues online for the first time.

On Jan. 25, 2007, TSCPA held its third CPA Ambassador Program at Society headquarters. Vic Alexander, Lynn Battles, Andy Bonner, Patricia Conry Taylor, Deborah Jones, Jenneen Kaufman, Sandra McClarty and Melissa Steagall-Jones participated in the daylong exercise.

On April 11, 2007, Gov. Phil Bredesen signed legislation that implemented the mobility provision of the UAA in Tennessee, the first state to do so. This provision eliminated the notification requirements for out-of-state CPAs practicing in Tennessee, and it subjected those CPAs to automatic jurisdiction in the state. Another aspect of the new law was the 200-day grace period for taking the CPA exam (the previous window was 120 days), which was the

Gov. Phil Bredesen signs legislation making Tennessee the first state in the nation to adopt the new uniform mobility standards to ease restrictions on CPA mobility between states. Similar legislation was subsequently passed in nearly all states. Witnessing the signing ceremony were, from left: Vic Alexander, CPA, Chair of the Tennessee State Board of Accountancy; Will Pugh, CPA, Chair of the TSCPA Legislation Committee; and State Sen. Tim Burchett, sponsor of the legislation.

recommendation of the 120/150 task force. TSCPA supported both provisions.

April 27, 2007, was the date of the next meeting of the Board of Directors. A proposal to expand TSCPA headquarters was discussed at length. Steve Lieb made a motion to extend discussions with architects and to approve up to $72,000 to gather additional information. The motion was passed unanimously and would be presented to Council at its next meeting. Brad Floyd reported a concern that a Tennessee CPA firm wanted to advertise in the *Journal*. After discussion, the Board did not take a position on restricting advertising by CPA firms in the *Journal*.

Council met on July 16, 2007, at the Baytowne Wharf in Sandestin, Fla. President Wright updated the Council on Board and EMF actions since the last Council meeting. Brad Floyd presented members with a proposal from the Board of Directors to expand the TSCPA office building. A budget amendment of $900,000 for construction fees was passed unanimously. Contributions to the Educational and Memorial Foundation were made by the Memphis Chapter ($5,000), the Nashville Chapter ($10,000) and the West Tennessee Chapter ($12,500). The Society now had more than 8,000 members. The Board met on July 18, but no new business was discussed.

Wright considered approving the expansion of TSCPA headquarters and the passing of the mobility provision of the accountancy law as his most significant accomplishments during his time as president. He says, "I have always felt that no matter how much time I invested in our Society I have always received back more because of my involvement." Regarding the future, Wright feels that "the leadership of TSCPA/AICPA in the development of accounting standards for non-public companies is a very positive one that we should stay the course on."

The Board of Directors Workshop was held on Aug. 15-17 at the Marriott Shoals in Florence, Ala. The TSCPA president for the 2007-08 Society year was Janice Smith, of Knoxville. The Board approved Belmont University as the site for the high school

Accounting Academy for 2008 and 2009. Bob Harris led the group in a strategic planning session in order to update the 2004 TSCPA strategic plan. The Board re-affirmed the mission of the Society to "enhance the success of our members through service, support and advocacy." The group also approved a vision statement: "To be the premier professional organization serving all CPAs in Tennessee." Staff and volunteer activities were reviewed, with the focus being on how TSCPA could best serve its members. Before the Board would meet again, the economic climate in the country would change dramatically for the worse due to the economic crisis of 2007-08.

TSCPA President 2007-08
Janice B. Smith

The October 2007 issue of the *Tennessee CPA Journal* contained statistics about the increased involvement of women in the CPA profession. In 1952, there were 750 female CPAs in the United States; by 1972, the number had grown to 2,000. In 2007, according to an AICPA research report, there were 108,000 female CPAs in the United States. The research also showed that over half of accounting graduates in 2007 in the United States were female.

The number of CPA candidates continued to be an issue both nationally and in Tennessee, and the issue was now being referred to as the "CPA Pipeline." Members were urged to redouble their efforts to encourage graduates to sit for the CPA exam. The new format of the exam (computerization, more testing windows) was viewed as leading to procrastination and a lack of a sense of urgency for candidates. Leaders were concerned that as the baby boomers retired, there simply would not be enough CPAs to replace them. Firm partners and others in leadership roles were urged to encourage younger staff members to sit for the exam.

The Board of Directors met on Dec. 7, 2007, at Society headquarters. Brad Floyd updated the group on the building construction, and the

Board instructed the building task force to prepare a letter to chapters soliciting contributions and offering various naming rights for the office expansion. The strategic plan was reviewed, and the Board adopted the new vision statement for TSCPA: "To be the premier professional services organization serving all CPAs in Tennessee."

Interim Council met on Dec. 8. Brad Floyd was recognized for 30 years of service to TSCPA. Connie Rhea was also recognized by the group for her 25 years of service. President Smith reviewed the activity of the Board of Directors and the EMF since the last Council meeting. Council members broke into smaller groups to discuss the recently completed strategic plan and provide feedback on the plan.

Due to the ongoing construction at the TSCPA office, the Board of Directors met on April 25, 2008, at another Brentwood location. Brad Floyd provided an update on the building expansion. A proposed bylaw amendment was presented to the group. The proposal would change the titles of the chief elected officer (currently president) to "chair" and the chief staff executive to "president." This amendment was proposed to modernize TSCPA by better reflecting its current organizational structure. A second amendment to eliminate the requirement that associate members work under the supervision of a TSCPA member was presented. Both proposals were passed unanimously by the Board.

The Board was also updated on a staff project that tracked the previous attendees of the 2002-06 Accounting Academy programs. Letters had been sent to the participants, and of the students who responded, 56 percent were either currently majoring in or anticipated majoring in accounting in college. Another 17 percent were majoring in a related field such as finance or business.

By May 2008, 22 states had enacted legislation to adopt the mobility provision of the UAA. In addition, legislation was pending in 13 other states to do so. Michael Shmerling, of Nashville, was presented the AICPA Public Service Award at the May AICPA Council meeting. The AICPA Council also voted to designate the International Accounting Standards Board as an international accounting standards-setter. Many practitioners felt that International Financial Reporting Standards (IFRS) were coming sooner rather than later.

Janice Smith would consider the expansion of the TSCPA office, the formation of the Audit Committee, the financial literacy "Feed the Pig" program and the continuation of the AICPA Ambassador Program as major accomplishments during her tenure. She says, "The people in TSCPA make TSCPA what it has been, is now and will be in the future. It is sometimes easy to see an organization logo and forget that the logo represents people, not an entity. Personally, my experiences with TSCPA could not have been better and I gained so much more than I could ever give back."

> By May 2008, 22 states had enacted legislation to adopt the mobility provisions of the UAA. In addition, legislation was pending in 13 other states to do so.

Council met on July 17, 2008, at the Cool Springs Marriott in Franklin, Tenn. Brad Floyd updated the group on the building renovation and construction and stated the project should be completed by Aug. 31. The Council unanimously approved the bylaw amendment to change the titles of the chief elected officer and chief staff executive. The bylaw amendment regarding the associate member requirement was also unanimously passed. The Board of Directors, under the direction of the new chair, Mike Cain, of Brentwood, met briefly on July 18 to discuss the upcoming year.

TSCPA Chair 2008-09
R. Michael Cain

The Renaissance Ross Bridge Hotel in Birmingham, Ala., served as the site of the 2008 Board Workshop. Cynthia Lund, AICPA vice president, updated the group on initiatives being undertaken by the

Institute, including the CPA Pipeline, regulatory forces, international issues, financial literacy and other topics. Vic Alexander, Chair of the Tennessee State Board of Accountancy, and Mark Crocker, TSBA Executive Director, reviewed recent activities of the TSBA. They reported that the state board was transferring its peer review program to cover approximately 360 CPA firms to TSCPA. The results of a study to separate the TSBA into a semi-autonomous entity were provided. NASBA and the AICPA were studying a proposal to offer the CPA exam internationally. They stated that NASBA was getting encouragement to modify the UAA to allow the 120/150 plan, and that 22 states had already enacted this change. The Board discussed these issues with the state board representative but took no action on any of the proposals.

The Board approved a motion to adopt a "Code of Ethics and Conflict of Interest Policy" for the directors. In the Educational and Memorial Foundation meeting, the Board of Trustees approved a $25,000 contribution to be paid over the next five years to the AICPA Doctoral Student Program. This program had been developed by the AICPA to address the shortage of accounting professors nationwide. The goal of the program was to encourage professionals working in public accounting to pursue a career in academia by providing stipends to individuals seeking a doctorate degree.

At the April 24, 2009, meeting of the Board, Wendy Garvin, TSCPA's director of professional services, provided an update on the merger of the TSBA peer review program with that of TSCPA. The Board discussed the current TSBA rule on ethics CPE (four hours with one hour being Tennessee-specific) and voted to recommend to the State Board that the requirement be changed to two hours total with one hour being Tennessee-specific. The Board reviewed the guidelines of the Scholarship Committee in rewarding funds to students and passed two motions affecting these rules. First, students who are considered for scholarships must be U.S. citizens. Second, if students live out of state but attend a Tennessee school, they are eligible for a TSCPA scholarship if they meet their school's guidelines for in-state tuition.

The Council met on June 16, 2009, at the Grove Park Inn in Asheville, N.C. Chair Mike Cain called the group to order. Regular business was conducted, and no new business was discussed. The Board met briefly on June 17, 2009, at the Grove Park Inn. The only new item of business was to approve Belmont University as the host site for the 2010 and 2011 high school Accounting Academy.

The Board of Directors Workshop was held at The Lodge at Buckberry Creek in Gatlinburg on Aug. 5-7, 2009. The Board was led by Tom Hood in a strategic planning session that evaluated and re-affirmed the mission statement and vision of TSCPA. Members also discussed future opportunities for TSCPA in improving member service.

The economic crisis of 2007-08 was still affecting CPAs and their clients. Credit had been virtually frozen, and numerous businesses had closed. For the first time in memory, CPA firms had actually laid off employees. In just a year, the CPA Pipeline issue had disappeared. In response, TSCPA had created a recession toolkit that was available to members on the website. The toolkit was designed to assist CPAs in serving as valued advisors to their clients. The Society's Career Center was also available online for members looking for a job.

CHAPTER SEVEN
2009-2014

Developing the Next Generation

The Board of Directors met on Nov. 20, 2009, at Society headquarters. They discussed the results of the recently completed member survey. In November 2009, TSCPA had surveyed its members about a variety of professional issues, including the peer review transparency issue. A majority of members favored no change in the current system, meaning the results of CPA firms' peer reviews would remain confidential and would not be provided to the TSBA or other regulatory agencies. The Board agreed that no change should be proposed to amend the Accountancy Act to remove the confidentiality provisions.

The interim Council meeting occurred on Nov. 21, 2009. As usual, updates were given on legislative, AICPA and Board of Directors activities. Council members discussed the need for and timing of the fall interim Council meeting. After a lengthy discussion, the majority of the Council members agreed to continue the fall meeting and to incorporate more professional issues updates in the meeting. They also agreed the meeting should be scheduled two weeks before Thanksgiving.

In his chair's message in the January/February *Tennessee CPA Journal*, David Curbo, of Memphis, wrote about glimpses of a more optimistic economic outlook. He also mentioned a new AICPA-

TSCPA Chair 2009-10
David A. Curbo

created Blue Ribbon Panel to address the Private Company Financial Reporting issue. NASBA had joined the AICPA and the Financial Accounting Foundation in supporting accounting standards to meet the needs of private companies.

April 30, 2010, was the next meeting of the Board of Directors. Brad Floyd and Connie Rhea presented a proposal to update the Society's association management system. The Board amended the budget by $112,000 to update the system and to redesign TSCPA's website. The Trustees of the EMF unanimously approved a motion to change investment advisors for the foundation's endowment fund to Haws Goodwin Investment Management.

Council met on June 14, 2010, at the Chattanoogan Hotel. Normal business was conducted, but one new item was presented. On behalf of the Educational and Memorial Foundation, Chair Curbo announced the establishment of the Richard L. Townsend Scholarship Fund. This fund would be used to provide an annual scholarship to an outstanding Masters of Accountancy student at the University of Tennessee. Curbo also announced that Will Pugh had pledged to match funds given to a new scholarship fund up to $12,500. Council responded with a standing ovation for Mr. Pugh. The Board of Directors met briefly on June 16, 2010, under the new leadership of Andy Bonner, of Piney Flats. Chapter representatives provided updates on their activities, and no new business was introduced.

TSCPA Chair 2010-11
Jack A. "Andy" Bonner Jr.

The 2010 Board retreat was held at the MeadowView Marriott in Kingsport on Aug. 4-6. Chair Bonner welcomed the group to his former hometown. The

Board was updated on various initiatives that had been undertaken as a result of the strategic planning meeting held the previous August. The member survey had been completed, a young CPA task force had been appointed, the TSCPA software upgrade was underway, new webcasts and self-study vendors had been added for CPE delivery, and testimonies of past scholarship recipients ("Look at Me Now") had been included in each issue of the *Journal*.

The Board reviewed several proposed amendments to TSCPA Policies of Council and Bylaws. The proposal would allow student members to join TSCPA by paying a one-time initiation fee of $10. It also updated the language of the Bylaws to change the method of distributing information to members from the "membership newsletter" to the *Journal*. The proposal also addressed the issue of chapter-provided CPE. The policy had read that chapter programs "should not exceed four hours per day in duration," and the amendment proposal would change the rule to require that chapters not provide more than "30 hours per year" of CPE. All amendments were passed by the group.

On the second day of the workshop, Karen Hellmund, Knoxville Chapter Director, requested the Board revisit the amendment regarding chapter CPE. After a lengthy discussion, a motion was passed by a majority vote to change the policy from "30 hours per year" to "40 hours per year."

The trustees of the EMF also met during this time, and they unanimously approved designating $25,000 of the EMF endowment to create the Will J. Pugh Sr. Scholarship Award. Mr. Pugh had provided outstanding leadership and service to the profession and TSCPA for the last 42 years. This scholarship would be given annually to the top accounting student at the University of Tennessee who demonstrated outstanding leadership qualities as exemplified by Mr. Pugh.

The September/October issue of the *Tennessee CPA Journal* featured an article on TSCPA member Bruce Behn, an accounting professor at the University of Tennessee, Knoxville, who had been

Tennessee Gov. Bill Haslam met with TSCPA leaders during a meeting of the Nashville Chapter. From left are: Larry Morton, CPA; Brad Floyd, TSCPA President/CEO; Governor Haslam; Joseph Proctor, CPA; Sean Owens, CPA; and Danny Pressley, CPA.

appointed to serve on the Pathways Commission to Study the Future of Accounting Higher Education. The commission was formed as a joint effort of the AICPA and the American Accounting Association to examine a series of issues facing higher education at the time, including a shortage of qualified teachers with doctorate degrees, the need to revise accounting curricula, university budget constraints and the need for specialized training to meet the profession's demand.

The Board met on Nov. 12, 2010, at TSCPA headquarters. A motion to change student membership dues from $25 annually to a one-time fee of $10 was passed unanimously. Board members also discussed the council policy concerning chapter CPE. A motion was passed by a majority vote to change the policy to "programs should not exceed four hours in duration" from the previous policy at that time, which had read "programs should not exceed four hours per day in duration."

Council met the next day and approved the changes in student fee and chapter CPE policies. David Morgan presented an update on

Private Company Financial Reporting, the preparer tax identification number (PTIN) requirement and tax return preparer registration.

In early 2011, the AICPA and the London-based Chartered Institute of Management Accountants (CIMA) announced they were exploring the development of a new international designation for management accountants. This proposal would demonstrate a combined competency and expertise in management accounting and global financial and business management.

> The trustees of the EMF unanimously approved designating $25,000 of the EMF endowment to create the Will J. Pugh Sr. Scholarship Award, given annually to the top accounting student at the University of Tennessee who demonstrated outstanding leadership qualities as exemplified by Mr. Pugh.

In March 2011, the AICPA announced it was going to update the results of the Vision Project from 1998 with a new initiative: Horizons 2025. This time, however, there would be no future forums; the entire process would be undertaken via technology. Members were asked to complete an online survey in order to determine the next chapter of the profession's vision. The results of the members' responses re-affirmed the findings of the original project, and little fanfare was made of them as compared to 1998.

Chair Andy Bonner presided at the April 29, 2011, Board of Directors meeting. The main point of discussion was related to the new association management software. Bonner reported that the project had experienced unanticipated delays in the software development phase. Staff would continue to support the development of the software and would keep the Board informed of the progress of the project. Wendy Garvin provided an update on the peer review program. The Board voted to award the 2012 high school Accounting Academy to Lipscomb University.

The last few years had seen the development of social networking, and TSCPA had incorporated this technology into its member service areas. Members could "like" TSCPA on Facebook, "follow" it on Twitter or join the Society's LinkedIn group. Social networking was being used by Society staff to inform members of new developments and upcoming events. QR codes were also introduced for downloading the *Tennessee CPA Journal* digital edition.

The Tennessee State Board of Accountancy made several rule changes that were summarized in the July/August *Journal*. Graduate courses taken by students would no longer count as 1.5 credit hours (a graduate course had counted as 4.5 hours in determining a candidate's required total of 150 hours). The education requirement to qualify to sit for the CPA exam was also changed to require only 24 hours in accounting (the previous requirement had been 30 hours). The ethics CPE requirement of four total hours with one hour of Tennessee-specific ethics each renewal period would be changed in January 2012 to require two hours of ethics that were Tennessee-specific each two years.

TSCPA Chair 2011-12
Katherine G. Watts

The Peabody Hotel was the site of the June 12, 2011, Council meeting. Nominations were made, the budget was approved, and updates on Board and EMF activities were presented. Ernie Baugh provided an update on the Blue Ribbon Panel on Private Company Financial Reporting and the importance of the group's findings. New chair Kathy Watts, of Brownsville, called the Board of Directors meeting to order on June 14, and no new business was presented.

The Board of Directors Workshop was held on Aug. 4-5 at the Inn at Biltmore Estates in Asheville, N.C. Kara Fitzgerald was introduced as TSCPA's new Director of Finance. Mark Koziel, AICPA Director of Specialized Communities and Firm Practice Management, provided an update on AICPA activities. Koziel spoke about financial accounting standards for private companies, Public Company Accounting Oversight Board activities, IFRS, the international offering of the CPA exam and the chartered global management accountant credential (CGMA). The CGMA was the outcome of the joint venture of the AICPA and CIMA.

The workshop continued, with the Board addressing other issues. A motion was passed unanimously that Chair Watts submit a letter to the Financial Accounting Foundation (FAF) expressing TSCPA's support of the recommendations of the Blue Ribbon Panel to improve reporting requirements for private companies. The Board discussed the problems with the new association management software, and a motion was passed to continue using the Society's current software for the next two years. The council policy regarding convention

The 22nd annual Autumn Children's Festival was held Oct. 1-2, 2011, at Chattanooga Riverpark. It raised $56,491 for the Chattanooga area Ronald McDonald House. Over the years, the Chattanooga Chapter has raised over $600,000 through the event.

planning was amended to reduce the time to approve the geographic area and the specific venue for future conventions.

On Oct. 4, 2011, the Financial Accounting Foundation announced that it would establish a Private Company Standards Improvement Council to identify, propose and vote on specific improvements to accounting principles for private businesses. This announcement was not in line with the AICPA's Blue Ribbon Panel, which had asked for autonomy in the process. The PCSIC would be subject to FASB approval, and the Blue Ribbon Panel felt as if FASB oversight would hinder the standard-setting process. In response, the AICPA Board of Directors was prepared to create a separate standard-setting body.

NASBA and the AICPA launched a website, *www.cpamobility.org*, to assist practitioners in determining mobility requirements in the various CPA jurisdictions. Practitioners could use the site to determine if they could work across state lines without any additional licensing or notice issues.

The Board met on Nov. 18, 2011, at Society headquarters. Board members participated in the FAF webcast that summarized the group's intentions with regard to Private Company Financial reporting. The Board then voted unanimously to send a letter to FAF and ask the group to establish an independent standard-setting body not subject to FASB oversight. Chair Watts updated the group on other AICPA activities.

TSCPA headquarters was the site of the Nov. 19, 2011, meeting of Council. Mark Koziel of the AICPA presented "Change Vision Opportunity for the Future" to the members.

Chair Watts reviewed the Board of Directors' activities since the last Council meeting. Andy Bonner made a motion that a unified letter from the TSCPA Council and Board of Directors be sent to the FAF. The letter would urge FAF to establish a new, independent standard-setting body for private companies. The motion was passed by Council unanimously. Council also unanimously approved the change to the policy concerning the identification of future convention sites.

On May 4, 2012, the Board of Directors met at Society headquarters. The group discussed the upcoming review of the State Board of Accountancy's independent structure, and Chair Watts appointed a task force to review and monitor the proceedings. Brad Floyd and Connie Rhea updated the Board on the required technology enhancements for the short-term and long-term needs of the Society. Wendy Garvin presented an update on the TSCPA peer review program and the State Board.

According to TSCPA membership statistics, in 2012, women made up more than 50 percent of TSCPA membership under the age of 40. To address issues faced by female CPAs, TSCPA held its first Women's Career Summit at Society headquarters in May 2012. The event provided locally and nationally known speakers who addressed issues and offered insights to women in the profession.

Council met at the Omni Amelia Island Plantation in Florida on June 12, 2012. Chair Watts updated the group on Board of Directors and EMF activities. No new business was discussed.

The Board of Directors Workshop was held Aug. 1-3, 2012, at Barnsley Gardens Resort in Adairsville, Ga. Chair David Haddock, of Brentwood, led the meeting. Board members discussed Life Member qualifications but deferred any action until the November meeting. Brad Floyd provided an update of recent activities of the Tennessee State Board of Accountancy. The Board requested the formation of an ad hoc committee to create a proposal on the continuance of the state board and work with the commissioner of the Department of Commerce & Insurance before seeking legislation.

TSCPA Chair 2012-13
M. David Haddock Jr.

The majority of the Board Workshop was a strategic planning session led by Jody Lentz. Lentz used the book *Race for Relevance*, by Harrison Coerver and Mary Byers, as the foundation for the session.

Both authors had extensive experience in consulting for association boards. The book calls for radical change that association boards must take in order to remain relevant in the future given changing technology and member demographics. These changes included overhauling the governance model and committee operations, empowering the CEO and enhancing staff expertise, rigorously defining the member market, rationalizing programs and services, and building a robust technology framework.

> According to TSCPA membership statistics, in 2012, women made up more than 50 percent of TSCPA membership under the age of 40. To address issues faced by female CPAs, TSCPA held its first Women's Career Summit at Society headquarters in May 2012.

The Board had lengthy conversations during the session about the possible relationship of the material covered by Lentz and TSCPA's current governance system, programs and services. The main focus of the discussion focused on the roles of Council and the Board of Directors in leading the organization. The bylaws stated the Council was the governing body of the Society. However, attendance at Council meetings had declined to the point that at the June 12, 2012, meeting, only 34 of the 119 members were present. In addition, except for a few items over the last 30 years, Council had turned over the governing role to the Board of Directors. No action was taken at the workshop with regard to these issues, but the issue would continue to receive Board attention in the future.

Given the discussion about the role of Council at the Board Workshop, TSCPA staff conducted a survey of Council members in September 2012. The brief survey was emailed to the 116 members of Council, and 54 members responded (46.6 percent). The survey asked members, "Is Council still relevant as TSCPA's governing body?", "Should the format or frequency of Council meetings be changed?", and "Should Council consider changing TSCPA's governing structure?" The results of the survey were mixed, and no action was taken by either the Board of Directors or Council at that time.

The Board of Directors met on Nov. 8, 2012, at the Society offices. Chair Haddock and Kevin Hickman, Chair-elect, updated the group on AICPA activities. Wendy Garvin presented a report from the Professional Ethics Committee that highlighted some differences between TSCPA and AICPA bylaws with respect to automatic termination of members when certain ethics violations occurred. The Board requested further study of the issue. Board members also reviewed a draft of a definition of "valuable service" guidelines for Life Members. No action was taken, but a task force to review the issue would be formed.

At the EMF Board of Trustees meeting on the same day, Brad Floyd updated the group on the creation of a new scholarship fund

The Memphis Chapter volunteered to help at the first water stop for the St. Jude full and half marathon on Dec. 1, 2012, in Memphis. The chapter has a long history of providing support and contributions to the St. Jude Children's Hospital.

Calvin A. and Jean C. King

that was being developed with the financial support of the Calvin A. King & Jean C. King Charitable Foundation.

Council met on Nov. 9, 2012, at the Society office. David Morgan, Chair of the AICPA Financial Reporting Framework for Small and Medium-Sized Entities Task Force, updated the members on the group's progress. Jody Lentz presented "Creative People Must Be Stopped: 6 Ways We Kill Innovation (Without Even Trying)" to Council. Council members were broken into small groups to discuss the relevancy of Council. Reports of each group were presented to Council. Council unanimously voted to adopt a new Board policy on admission to membership and deleted the Council policy about the same issue. Brad Floyd updated Council members about the Calvin A. King & Jean C. King Charitable Foundation Scholarship Program.

In January, TSCPA announced that the King Charitable Foundation would become a major benefactor of the Educational and Memorial Foundation. Mr. King had served as Memphis Chapter president, a member of Council and the Board of Directors, and as TSCPA president in 1983-84. This donation would allow the EMF, beginning in 2013, to award $100,000 to $150,000 in additional scholarship awards to students in Tennessee. This program would essentially double the scholarship effort of the EMF. As of today, the EMF has awarded over $3 million in scholarships to accounting students in Tennessee.

The Memphis firm Reynolds, Bone & Griesbeck honored Ray Kamler, 1988-89 TSCPA president, with a generous donation to the EMF. Kamler was named a Benefactor of the foundation's Life

Associate Program in recognition of his lifetime service to the CPA profession.

On a sadder note, Axel Swang passed away on Jan. 8, 2013. He had served as the first executive secretary of TSCPA from 1957 to 1967, while also serving as department chair at David Lipscomb University. During his tenure, the Society had opened its first permanent office space and membership had grown from 456 to 772. In fact, because of this growth, the Board of Directors decided to replace the part-time executive secretary position with a full-time position (filled by Ted Moody).

In the January/February issue of the *Tennessee CPA Journal*, David Morgan was interviewed about the newly released AICPA proposal on accounting standards for private companies. After FASB rejected the findings of the Blue Ribbon Panel (on which Morgan had served), the AICPA formed a committee to develop their own set of standards. Morgan had served as chair of this committee. The exposure draft of these standards, Financial Reporting Framework for Small and Medium-Sized Entities (FRF for SMEs), had been released.

The Board of Directors met on April 26, 2013, at the Society office in Brentwood. Board members discussed the qualifications for Life Members and considered an amendment to section 2.3 of the bylaws. The amendment would eliminate the required "valuable service" criteria and provide that fellow members in good standing for at least 45 years would automatically qualify as Life Members. After a lengthy discussion, the Board unanimously approved a change in membership classifications and the dues structure to a simplified system based upon the years a member had been certified.

Aleshia Garrett, TSCPA director of marketing and communications, updated the Board on the new communication initiatives, including the new digital *Journal* mobile app and video production. The Board accepted proposed recommendations from the Professional Ethics Committee that would amend TSCPA policy to mirror that of the AICPA. This revision would allow TSCPA to take action without a hearing if a member had already been sanctioned through automatic provisions.

On June 24, 2013, the TSCPA Scholarship Committee met and awarded $250,575 to 119 college/university students across the state. This represented a 95 percent increase in the amount of scholarship funds from the previous year. The increase was due to the generous contribution of the Calvin & Jean King Foundation, which allowed the committee to award four recipients with $25,000 scholarships over their college tenure, in addition to the "normal" scholarships.

On June 26, 2013, a conference call was held by the Board of Directors in order to adopt a resolution in support of FRF for SMEs. Following a lengthy discussion of the issue, the Board unanimously supported the framework. The TSBA would officially recognize FRF for SMEs as an accepted reporting framework on July 19, an announcement reported by Brad Floyd via Twitter.

> On June 24, 2013, the TSCPA Scholarship Committee awarded $250,575 to 119 college students across the state, a 95 percent increase from the previous year. This was due to the generous contribution of the Calvin & Jean King Foundation, which allowed the committee to award four recipients with $25,000 scholarships over their college tenure.

David Haddock would later reflect on his year as chair by stating, "When I think of TSCPA, I see faces of people that I would never have known if not for the association. Conventions across our state and region are also very special memories. Thank you TSCPA for being the torchbearer of our profession in Tennessee!"

The July meeting of Council was held at the Renaissance Hotel in Nashville on July 18. Bill Balhoff, AICPA Chair-elect, provided a professional issues update to the group. Chair Haddock recommended that Council adopt the bylaws amendment regarding Life Members. A motion to approve the amendment was made. After discussion, a motion was made to table the issue, which passed with a majority vote. Per the Professional Ethics Committee's recommendations, a motion to amend TSCPA's bylaws to mirror those of the AICPA and allow TSCPA to take action without a hearing if a member had already been sanctioned though automatic provisions was passed by a majority vote. Haddock presented the Board's proposal to revise the current dues structure and membership classification structure of the Society. This motion was passed by Council. The Board of Directors met on July 19, 2013, with Kevin Hickman, of Nashville, assuming the role of chair.

TSCPA Chair 2013-14
Kevin E. Hickman

The Board Workshop for 2013 was held at the Grove Park Inn in Asheville, N.C., on Aug. 11-13. After conducting the normal course of business, the Board discussed the requirements for Life Members. The discussion focused on the definition of "valuable service" as one of the criteria for Life Membership. The group unanimously approved an amendment to the board policy that stated, "Valuable service for Life Membership shall be - nominees must have served on the TSCPA Board of Directors or served as a TSCPA chapter president."

On Nov. 7, 2013, the Board of Directors met at TSCPA headquarters. Chair Hickman convened the meeting to order. The Board reviewed a proposal from staff to implement a centralized record-keeping system. The purpose of this system was to allow TSCPA staff to provide chapter services such as cash disbursements, cash receipts, bank reconciliation and financial statement preparation at no cost. The proposal would eliminate the need for the individual chapters to have an annual audit. A motion to approve the proposal was passed by a majority vote, and the Board recommended that chapters adopt the system by March 31, 2014, in order to ensure uniform compliance.

Board members reviewed and discussed a proposed succession plan for the TSCPA President/CEO that had been prepared by the Personnel Committee. A motion was passed to adopt the plan, with the understanding that it would be reviewed annually at the Board Workshop.

The Board also heard a proposal from the National Association of State Boards of Accountancy about a CPE audit service program. This program would provide outsourced services to the state boards to help manage their CPE audits of licensees. The TSCPA Board took no action on this proposal.

The interim Council meeting took place on Nov. 8, 2013. Harrison Coerver presented "The New Normal for Professional Societies: Governance Consequences" to the group. Council members broke into small groups to discuss the biggest opportunities and challenges for TSCPA in the next five years. They also discussed what competencies, characteristics, skills and attributes the Society needed on the Board of Directors given those opportunities and challenges. The Council reconvened, and a lengthy discussion followed. No formal action was taken on this item.

Chair Kevin Hickman convened the quarterly meeting of the Board of Directors to order on May 2, 2014, at TSCPA headquarters. Kara Fitzgerald, CFO, updated the members on member renewal and retention activities. She discussed the 2014-15 Membership Development Plan, which included a Young CPA Workgroup. The workgroup will be comprised of young CPA thought leaders from across the state, with the goal of engaging, connecting and building unity among young CPA members.

Treasurer Charles Groves reported that all chapters except Elk Valley had adopted the centralized record-keeping system. Doug Warren provided an update on the AICPA initiative The Future of Learning. This program had been developed to determine the major

TSCPA members met with U.S. Senators Lamar Alexander and Bob Corker during the 2013 AICPA Annual Meeting in Washington, D.C. From left are: Arthur L. Sparks Jr., CPA, of Union City; Jack A. "Andy" Bonner, CPA, of Piney Flats; Sen. Lamar Alexander; Sen. Bob Corker; R. Michael Cain, CPA, of Brentwood; and Kevin E. Hickman, CPA, of Nashville.

trends in education and the impact these trends could have on the future of the CPA profession, especially in the delivery of CPE. A task force of public accounting leaders, industry CPAs, regulators, association leaders and educators had been formed by the AICPA and had spent the last year studying this issue.

Connie Rhea, COO, reported that the Society had developed a CPE Tracker for members to use. This system allowed members to view all educational events purchased through TSCPA and to add outside events to the Tracker, assisting members in compiling their CPE hours in the event of a State Board audit.

Council met in its regular meeting on June 8, 2014, at the MeadowView Conference Resort and Convention Center in Kingsport. Kevin Hickman, Chair, presided over the meeting. Hickman provided an update on Board and EMF activities since the last Council meeting. Nominations for Society officers and EMF trustees were unanimously passed by the group. Art Sparks, Chair-elect, gave a presentation on "Building the Profession of Tomorrow Reinforcing the Profession's Commitment to Quality." Doug Warren updated Council on The Future of Learning program.

The Board of Directors met on June 10 at MeadowView. Chair Art Sparks of Union City called the meeting to order. Chapter presidents and presidents-elect were present at the meeting and provided updates on their respective chapters' activities.

TSCPA Chair 2014-15
Arthur L. Sparks Jr.

The Board workshop was held on Aug. 3-5, 2014, at Barnsley Gardens in Adairsville, Ga., with Chair Art Sparks leading the group. David Morgan, AICPA Board of Directors member, provided an update on professional issues and AICPA activities. These activities included The Future of Learning, advocacy issues, student initiatives, changes to the UAA, diversity programs and technology changes.

Mark Crocker, Executive Director of the Tennessee State Board of Accountancy, and Henry Hoss, State Board member, attended the meeting to provide an update on State Board initiatives. Of particular interest was the desire of the State Board to remove the confidentiality provisions contained in the accountancy law regarding the peer review program administered by TSCPA. After a lengthy discussion, the TSCPA Board did not approve the proposal to support an amendment to remove peer review confidentiality, and decided to see if the newly formed Peer Review Oversight Committee would address the State Board's concerns.

Board members broke into three groups to discuss strategic planning. Chapter reports, committee reports and TSCPA staff reports were given. The group discussed the past year's convention and a location for future conventions. Board and Council bylaws were discussed, and minor revisions were passed to be presented to Council in November.

The Board of Directors met on November 6, 2014, at TSCPA headquarters in Brentwood. Chair Art Sparks and Charles Groves, Chair-elect, provided a report on the recent AICPA Council meeting. Richard Hill, a member of the ACIPA Peer Review Committee, addressed the group about the peer review confidentiality provision contained in the Tennessee rules and regulations. Hill informed the Board that Tennessee was one of only four states that had this provision, and he felt the rules should be revised to allow the State Board to have access to the results of the TSCPA-administered peer review program. The Board discussed this proposal and decided to address the issues at the meeting of Council the next day. Other normal business items were approved by the group.

Council met on Nov. 7, 2014, at headquarters. Mandy Young, TSCPA lobbyist, provided an update on the recent state elections to the group and the possible effect of the elections on the business climate in the state. Chair Sparks updated Council with an overview of TSCPA operations. Council approved an amendment to Council Policy No. 1, which revised the membership classifications of the Society.

Bill Blaufuss, Chair of the TSBA, spoke to the group about recent changes with the Board of Accountancy. A group panel was convened consisting of Blaufuss, Mark Crocker, Richard Hill and Wendy Garvin to discuss the peer review confidentiality issue. After a lengthy discussion, Council was broken into several discussion groups to address the pros and cons of the peer review confidentiality issue. The spokesperson for each group presented the results of the discussions, and the general consensus on the topic was split. The Council did not act upon the proposal to remove peer review confidentiality provisions contained in the Tennessee Accountancy Law, and the issue will be further addressed at future Board and Council meetings.

TSCPA Chair 2015-16
Charles F. Groves III

David Morgan, member of the AICPA Board of Directors, provided an update on AICPA activities to Council. The Future of Learning initiative was highlighted by Morgan. The institute is moving forward quickly on the program, which features nano-learning, using the cloud, collaboration and curriculum development. The Future of Learning would measure competency, not seat time, in awarding continuing professional education. As this program is developed and possibly implemented in the near future, the Society will have to be proactive in the delivery and content of its CPE offerings.

In 2014, TSCPA celebrated its 110th year as the premier professional organization serving all CPAs in Tennessee. As of Dec. 31, 2014, the Society had a total membership of 9,444, making it the 15th-largest state CPA society in the country, and 904 CPA firms in Tennessee were enrolled in the Peer Review Program. The Society awarded over $350,000 in scholarships in 2014, and the Educational & Memorial Foundation hosted over 300 seminars, conferences and other CPE opportunities for members throughout the state.

TSCPA continues to represent the CPA profession before legislative and regulatory bodies whose actions directly impact the profession. Aided by the Tennessee CPA Political Action Committee, the Society actively supports good government and serves as a valuable resource to lawmakers and standard-setters. Through the outstanding leadership of volunteers at the state and chapter levels, as well as the dedication and professionalism of TSCPA staff, the Society has grown into one of the leading state societies in the United States.

Summary, Conclusions and Observations

Over the time covered by this book, the CPA profession has faced growth, opportunity and turmoil. A lot has changed in society since 1978, and the driving force has been technology. Today's generation has been born into the second great societal revolution: the Technology Age. Just as the Industrial Revolution influenced society, so has the Technology Age.

The Industrial Revolution changed America from an agricultural, rural society into one that was urban and industrialized. This revolution created an enormous demand for accounting as corporations were formed and manufacturing expanded. The need for external financial reporting was created as stockholders, no longer privy to inside corporate information, demanded an annual report concerning their investment. The required assurance on these reports created the need for external, independent auditors. Generally Accepted Accounting Principles, auditing standards and Rules of Professional Conduct had to be developed. Manufacturers implemented cost accounting rules in order to understand and control these costs. Societal changes had resulted in enormous demand for accountants and auditors.

The exponential growth of technology has not been a focus of this book. A few references were made to illustrate the state of technology as time passed. Each of us of a certain age can remember the time of phone booths (replaced by cell phones), 15-column green work papers (Excel) and going to a library to research a paper (the Internet). Technology has improved our lives (most of the time) and will continue to evolve in the future.

The future of the accounting profession appears promising; however, CPAs will have to continue to adapt to technological advances in order to remain relevant and in societal demand. In late 2013, the Intuit 2013 Future of Accountancy Report was released. This report summarized the impact of demographic, economic, social and technological trends on the profession over the next decade. The profession will be reshaped as cloud computing, advanced analytical tools, large data sets and social and mobile computing continue to advance. These productivity advancements will change the focus of accounting from computation into consulting as clients and employers demand more information and advice from their CPAs. Real-time, online support will be required in order to satisfy client demands, and mobile devices will allow accountants to interact virtually with clients from any place at any time. The world has become connected, and the "Internet of everything" is the latest trend that will dramatically change how we live.

CPAs will have to embrace the technology advancement that will continue to change how businesses and individuals operate in the future. Many CPA firms have kept up with the revolution, but they will have to continue their commitment to this trend.

Several issues must also be resolved in order for TSCPA to maintain its prominence and relevance in the future. Obtaining and involving young, new members must remain a priority. TSCPA must make every effort to embrace the rapid pace of technological change, as younger generations, which have grown up with technology, expect any group with which they are associated be on the leading edge of technology.

Lastly, the pipeline issue must be brought back into discussion. The number of accounting graduates has returned to pre-2007 levels, but the number of individuals passing the exam has not increased. CPA firms, employers and educators must recommit to the importance of stressing to graduates the value of the CPA. The demographics of TSCPA members shows that our membership is aging, and new accounting graduates must pass the exam and become members of the Society in the future. In addition, the profession must find ways to retain new CPAs.

It has been 37 years since the first history of the Society, *History of the Tennessee Society of Certified Public Accountants, 1904-1977*, was published. If TSCPA waits that amount of time before issuing another history after this one, it will be the year 2051. The author of that book will surely feel nostalgic about the technology of this time and the more simple society in which we currently live. He or she will smile about the fact this book was typed, communicated through email and probably actually printed on paper. What will TSCPA be in 2051? Hopefully a thriving, vibrant organization that still "Enhances the Success of our Members through Service, Support and Advocacy."

APPENDIX I

2015-16 TSCPA Board of Directors

Chair
Charles F. Groves III, CPA
Chattanooga

Chair-elect
Sondra T. Harris-Webb, CPA
Collierville

Vice Chair
Anita Hamilton, CPA
Jackson

Secretary
Barrett Simonis, CPA
Knoxville

Treasurer
Douglas E. Warren, CPA
Sweetwater

Past Chair
Arthur L. Sparks Jr., CPA
Union City

At-large Member (2015-2018)
Jenneen Kaufman, CPA
Nashville

At-large Member (2014-2017)
Jeremy L. Nichols, CPA
Franklin

At-large Member (2014-2016)
Mark E. Steadman, CPA
Johnson City

*Appalachian Chapter
Director (2013-2016)*
Betty J. Sotherland, CPA
Johnson City

*Chattanooga Chapter
Director (2014-2017)*
Christian E. Bennett, CPA
Chattanooga

*Elk Valley Chapter
Director (2014-2017)*
Beverly E. Saylor, CPA
Shelbyville

*Knoxville Chapter
Director (2015-2018)*
Benjamin M. Alexander, CPA
Knoxville

*Memphis Chapter
Director (2013-2016)*
Mark W. McBryde, CPA
Germantown

*Nashville Chapter
Director (2014-2017)*
H. Rowan Leathers III, JD, CPA
Nashville

*Upper Cumberland Chapter
Director (2015-2018)*
Thomas G. Janney, CPA
Smithville

*West Tennessee Chapter
Director (2015-2018)*
John D. Whybrew, CPA
Jackson

APPENDIX II

2015-16 TSCPA Staff

President/CEO
Brad Floyd

Chief Operating Officer
Connie Rhea

Chief Financial Officer
Kara Fitzgerald

Director of Marketing
& Communications
Aleshia Garrett

Director of Professional
Services
Wendy Garvin

Director of Professional
Development
Christine Sharp

Conference & Events
Manager
Jamie Compton

Member Engagement
Manager
Ashley Beil

Graphic Designer
Lindsey Baldwin

*Communications/
Technology Associate*
Jared Booth

*Chapter & Member
Services Associate*
Cassidy Carlgren

*Membership Services
Associate*
Katie Cheek

Data Integrity Associate
Amanda Davis

*Business Development
Associate*
Kate Gurevich

Staff Accountant
Dena Jackson

*Accounting Services
Associate*
Kristin Lawrence

*Video Production
Associate*
Lorin Kee

Receptionist
Carolyn Lynn

Meetings Associate
Jennifer Webb

*Peer Review Technical
Consultant*
Roger Johnson

APPENDIX III

Chapter Presidents

Appalachian Chapter

1978 Dwight Leonard
1979 Loren Plucker
1980 Robert Neal
1981 Thomas McKee
1982 Cathy Peters
1983 William Moss
1984 Don Royston
1985 Buddy Yonz
1986 Elizabeth Lunsford
1987 Lee Davis Jr.
1988 Richard Linnen
1989 Ellen Barnett
1990 Andy Bonner Jr.

1991 Mickey Ellis
1992 Steven Hale
1993 Charles Huffman
1994 David Frizzell
1995 Tony Jennings
1996 Thomas Greer
1997 Douglas Blackley
1998 Margaret Moses
1999 Mark Steadman
2000 Billy Gilliam
2001 Whitney Ball
2002 Sherry Grygotis
2003 Gail Taylor

2004 Melissa Steagall-Jones
2005 Jonathan Bailey
2006 John Malone
2007 Betty Sotherland
2008 Jason M. Edmisten
2009 Rebecca Cox
2010 Donna Jones
2011 James Andy Hatfield
2012 Deanna Griffith
2013 Sharon Bryant
2014 Misty Turnbull
2015 Ben Buchanan

Chattanooga Chapter

1978 Melvin Young
1979 Larry Page
1980 Jerry Adams
1981 Brice Holland
1982 Betty Chadwick
1983 Erhardt Barnes
1984 Ralph Kendall
1985 Lee Gurley III
1986 Martin Orr
1987 Gordon Guilbert
1988 Billy Cordell
1989 Casey Stuart
1990 John Houston

1991 David Young III
1992 Steele Jones
1993 Robert Rabon
1994 Henry Hoss
1995 Louis Wright
1996 Ernest Baugh Jr.
1997 Becky Sue Warren
1998 Lawrence Stone Jr.
1999 Terri Jeter-McAvoy
2000 Charles Groves III
2001 David Haddock Jr.
2002 Robin Shields
2003 Michael Costello

2004 Brantley Mason
2005 Lynn Battles
2006 Renee B. Ford
2007 Salvatore Garaci
2008 Joyce Kendall
2009 Rebecca Fingerle
2010 Thomas Gavin
2011 Kim Lawrence
2012 Tony D'Andrea
2013 Christian Bennett
2014 Jerome England
2015 Jeffrey Ross

Elk Valley Chapter

1989 Coyle Clark
1990 Gary Hunt
1991 Bryan Bean
1992 Barry Cooper
1993 Robert Knies
1994 John Robertson
1995 Paul Young
1996 Betty Sue Hussey
1997 Rush Bricken
1998 Christopher Bell
1999 Robert Daniel
2000 Ward Harder
2001 Donald Ellis Jr.
2002 Betty Sue Hussey
2003 Cameron Ray
2004 Gary Hunt
2005 Ward Harder
2006 Rush Bricken
2007 Paul Young
2008 Beverly Saylor
2009 Ward Harder
2010 Betty Sue Hussey
2011 Fayna Sargent
2012 Fayna Sargent
2013 Fayna Sargent
2014 Holly Wade
2015 Holly Wade

Knoxville Chapter

1978 Samuel Coulter
1979 David Bolton
1980 Robert Pratt
1981 Ronald Justus
1982 Willard Carr
1983 Allen Knable
1984 Janet Leming
1985 Virginia Morrow
1986 Edgar Gee Jr.
1987 Donna Terzak
1988 Larry Elmore
1989 Steven Harb
1990 Van Elkins
1991 Daniel Pressley
1992 James Myers
1993 Douglas Izard
1994 Greg Gilbert
1995 Jesse Hammond
1996 Gregg Woodall
1997 James Lloyd
1998 Samuel Letsinger
1999 Janice Smith
2000 Deborah Diddle
2001 Scott Dotson
2002 Karen Hellmund
2003 Donald Foraker Jr.
2004 Brian Tankersley
2005 Bryan Dove
2006 Lee Sherbakoff
2007 Mike Heffner
2008 Linda Jo Pomerance
2009 John Kirk
2010 Ben Alexander
2011 Thomas Booker
2012 F. Edwin Lay
2013 Angela Godel
2014 Sean Brewer
2015 Laimon Godel Jr.

Memphis Chapter

1978 James Thompson
1979 Mack Browder
1980 Franklin Greer
1981 Art Svoboda
1982 Noris Rick Haynes Jr.
1983 William Frazee
1984 Lewis Holland
1985 Mickey Ison
1986 Raymond Kamler
1987 Michael Uiberall
1988 Paul Brundige
1989 William Griesbeck
1990 Vicki Dunn
1991 Jerry Allison
1992 Raymond Butler Jr.
1993 David Cuicchi
1994 George Barber III
1995 Marie Dubke
1996 Robbie McKinney
1997 John Trusty
1998 Sandra Zehntner
1999 John Schifani
2000 John Griesbeck
2001 David Curbo
2002 Shelley Smith
2003 Steven Leib
2004 Terry Stanford
2005 Dan Work Jr.
2006 Victor Butcher
2007 Sudhir Agrawal
2008 Robert Vance Jr.
2009 Ted Showalter
2010 Brian McCuller
2011 Ginny Szalay
2012 Sonda Harris-Webb
2013 Mark McBryde
2014 William Gillaspie
2015 Cherry Blanton

Nashville Chapter

1978 Gary Loyd
1979 Thomas Burgess
1980 Darrel Tongate
1981 Patricia Williams
1982 Sam Hirshberg
1983 Fred Frick
1984 Lee Kraft
1985 Albert White
1986 Charles Frasier
1987 Charles Dennard
1988 Wynne Baker
1989 Jack Elisar
1990 Michael Shmerling

1991 Richard Schell
1992 Timothy Rhodes
1993 James Jamieson
1994 Albert Benneyworth
1995 Michael Scarlett
1996 David Morgan
1997 Al Kent IV
1998 Betty Price
1999 Bernard Goldstein
2000 Nina Hammontree
2001 Kathleen Zuccaro
2002 Robert Whisenant
2003 Nellie Ward-Cole

2004 Kevin Hickman
2005 Michael Cain
2006 Elizabeth Snider
2007 Charles Young
2008 Rowan Leathers
2009 Grant Smothers
2010 Crystal Shields
2011 Joseph Proctor
2012 Susanne Reseland
2013 Briana Mullenax
2014 Royce Rhea
2015 Amy Jamison

Upper Cumberland Chapter

1981 James Totherow
1982 Kenneth Draper
1983 Don Cook
1984 David Lynn
1985 Joe Thorne
1986 Larry Eldridge
1987 Orv Granade
1988 Marina Gore
1989 James Welch
1990 James Hawkins
1991 Edward Fuqua
1992 Carol Hamblen

1993 Thomas Janney
1994 G.A. Swanson
1995 Ronald Jarvis
1996 Orv Granade
1997 Raymond Johnson
1998 Jared Bennett
1999 Linda Leslie
2000 Barry Clouse
2001 Wade Montrief
2002 Stephen Boyd
2003 Barry Clouse
2004 Mohanlal Patel

2005 Kendra Alley
2006 Kendra Alley
2007 Barry Clouse
2008 Barry Clouse
2009 Kendra Saunders
2010 Dan Fesler
2011 Dan Fesler
2012 Dan Fesler
2013 Barry Clouse
2014 Barry Clouse
2015 Thomas Janney

West Tennessee Chapter

1978 Aubrey Carmichael
1979 James Dunn
1980 Robert Seabrook Jr.
1981 William Gillett
1982 Houston Payne III
1983 Winston Truett
1984 Arthur L. Sparks Jr.
1985 Michael Steele
1986 Robert Crenshaw
1987 Michael Hewitt
1988 Kevin Hunter
1989 James Shaw Jr.
1990 Kenneth Pierce

1991 Deborah Newell
1992 Randy Wallace
1993 Judith McKenzie
1994 Paul Hallock
1995 Richard Phebus
1996 Tom Copeland
1997 Kenneth Cozart
1998 Rex Baker
1999 Katherine Watts
2000 Judy Fletcher
2001 Charles Emrich
2002 Fancher Sargent
2003 Tom Carson Jones

2004 Trenton Watrous
2005 Barry Rich
2006 Laura Beth Butler
2007 John Whybrew
2008 Dan Walker
2009 Robert K. Cozart Jr.
2010 Stephen Eldridge
2011 T. Paul Anderson
2012 Karen Taylor
2013 Carrol Kessens
2014 Kevin McKenzie
2015 Brandon Lanciloti

APPENDIX IV

Convention Schedule

YEAR	HOST	LOCATION	HOTEL
1978	Chattanooga	Chattanooga	Choo-Choo Hilton
1979	Appalachian	Gatlinburg	Glenstone Lodge
1980	Memphis	Memphis	Hyatt Regency
1981	At-large	Hilton Head, S.C.	Hyatt on Hilton Head
1982	Nashville	Nashville	Opryland Hotel
1983	Knoxville	Knoxville	Hyatt Regency
1984	West Tennessee	Jackson	Civic Center
1985	Chattanooga	Chattanooga	Choo-Choo Hilton
1986	Appalachian	Gatlinburg	Park Vista
1987	At-large	Orlando, Fla.	Hyatt Regency-Grand Cypress
1988	Memphis	Memphis	Peabody
1989	Nashville	Nashville	Opryland Hotel
1990	Knoxville	Knoxville	Holiday Inn-World's Fair
1991	At-large	Bahamas	Carnival Cruise-Fantasy
1992	Appalachian	Gatlinburg	Glenstone Lodge
1993	Chattanooga	Chattanooga	Choo-Choo Hilton
1994	At-large	Panama City, Fla.	Marriott Bay Point Resort
1995	Memphis	Memphis	Peabody
1996	Nashville	Nashville	Opryland Hotel
1997	At-large	Asheville, N.C.	Grove Park Inn
1998	Knoxville	Knoxville	Hyatt Regency
1999	Appalachian	Kingsport	MeadowView Conference Center
2000	At-large	Lake Buena Vista, Fla.	Wyndam Palace Resort & Spa
2001	West Tennessee	Memphis	Adams Mark
2002	Nashville	Franklin	Cool Springs Marriott
2003	Chattanooga	Chattanooga	Chattanooga Marriott
2004	At-large	Isle of Palms, S.C.	Wild Dunes Resort
2005	Appalachian	Johnson City	Carnegie Hotel
2006	Memphis	Memphis	Peabody
2007	At-large	Destin, Fla.	Bay Towne Wharf
2008	Nashville	Franklin	Cool Springs Marriott
2009	Knoxville	Asheville, N.C.	Grove Park Inn
2010	Chattanooga	Chattanooga	Chattanoogan
2011	Memphis	Memphis	Peabody
2012	At-large	Amelia Island, Fla.	Amelia Island Plantation
2013	Nashville	Nashville	Renaissance Nashville
2014	Appalachian	Kingsport	MeadowView Conference Center
2015	Knoxville	Knoxville	Holiday Inn-World's Fair

CPSIA information can be obtained at www.ICGtesting.com
Printed in the USA
LVOW01s0539070515

437294LV00006B/7/P